L

LANDSCAPES OF WAR

FROM SARAJEVO TO CHECHNYA

Juan Goytisolo

Translated from the Spanish by Peter Bush
Introduction by Tariq Ali

CITY LIGHTS BOOKS SAN FRANCISCO

Cover design by Stefan Gutermuth
Cover photograph copyright © by George Azar
Reproduced by courtesy of George Azar

Book design by Robert Sharrard
Typography by Harvest Graphics

Library of Congress Cataloging-in-Publication Data

Goytisolo, Juan.
    Landscapes of war / by Juan Goytisolo ; translated by
Peter Bush.
        p.   cm.
    Chiefly a collection of previously published essays first
published in El País and then translated and published in
the Times.
    ISBN 0-87286-373-5 (pbk.)
    1. World politics — 1945 –   2. Violence — History — 20th
century.   3. Security, International.   4. Low intensity conflicts
(Military science) — History — 20th century.   5. Civil war.
6. Ethnic relations.   7. Military intervention.   I. Title.
D843.G69 2000
909.82'5—dc21   00-034642

CITY LIGHTS BOOKS are edited by Lawrence Ferlinghetti and
Nancy J. Peters and published at the City Lights Bookstore,
261 Columbus Avenue, San Francisco, CA 94133 Visit our
web site: www.citylights.com

CONTENTS

Chechnya

Approaches to Islam   203

ACKNOWLEDGMENTS

The essays, except for the final one, translated in this book were all written for *El País,* the Spanish daily newspaper. The series on Sarajevo were published there on 23–31 August 1993; on Algeria, 27 March–3 April 1994; on Palestine/Israel, 12–17 February 1995; on Chechnya, 1–7 July 1996. The general essay on Islam was first published in *Claves de la razón práctica,* Madrid, November 1994; *Cuadernos de Sarajevo* was published in book form, 1993; *Argelia en el vendaval,* 1994; *Paisajes de guerra con Chechenia al findo,* 1996; all by *El País*-Aguliar, Madrid. Extracts from the English translations have been published in the following London magazines: *The Times Literary Supplement, The New Statesman,* and *Casablanca.* The translator would like to thank Robert Fisk, Senada Kreso, and Anne McLean for their helpful comments.

INTRODUCTION

For nearly three decades now, Juan Goytisolo's war against conformity has been a beautiful and courageous thing to behold. He is a remarkable innovator but, unlike the fashionable gurus of the postmodern, Goytisolo reveres real history. He wages war against those—most mainstream currents in Western culture—who invent a false past, for he knows that in so doing they blight the future. His historico-literary excavations have had a tremendous impact on Spanish culture.

In his memoirs as well as his novels he has broken with many traditions—literary, historical, political, and social—discarding, in the process, the narrow, the primitive, the oppressive, and the irrational. The only weapon at his disposal has been the pen and he wields it with the skill of an old samurai warrior as the apologists in the Spanish Academy have often discovered to their cost.

Whereas Spanish readers can read Goytisolo regularly, often in the pages of *El País,* the provincial character of contemporary Anglophone culture deprives us of his observations on Islamic culture and society. Occasionally, an essay or a review appears in the *Times Literary Supplement,* followed by a long silence.

In *Saracen Chronicles**—a collection of his literary essays published in English in 1992—Goytisolo helped to unwind the common threads of Spanish and Latin American Literature showing how Arab culture was plundered, and often to good effect. In the concluding essay of that collection, "On Literature Considered as a Criminal Activity," Goytisolo explained his own literary project: ". . . as political, social, moral and sexual taboos disappear those subjects that are the object of a possible 'danger to society,' and the writer determined to resist the tremendous integrative force of the system finds

---

*Juan Goytisolo. *Saracen Chronicles.* Translated by Helen Lane. London: Quartet Books, 1992.

himself obliged to interiorize his provocation, introducing it into language itself."

The essays in this volume are an account of the war zones of the late twentieth century. The war waged by the French police against North African migrants in France and Palestine, the fate of the Bosnians after the breakup of Yugoslavia, the fratricidal frenzy in Algeria, and the wars in the Northern Caucasus. One eye is observational, the other analytic. Even where one disagrees with him, his argument never fails to stimulate.

As I write, there is hand-to-hand fighting in Grozny and the second war to occupy Chechnya is in progress. Rereading Goytisolo's description of the first war in this collection and his account of the history of the region indicates that the Russian hold is unlikely to be permanent.

On the scale of repression, the war in Chechnya is far worse than Milošević's campaign in Kosovo. More refugees have fled Grozny than ever did Pristina. But the Western media has, in general, averted its eyes from the conflict, proving that Kosovo was the war for NATO expansion and has very little to do with the real needs of the people of that region. Bosnia and Kosovo are NATO colonies run under the cover of the United Nations. Chechnya will become a Russian colony approved by the West. Ironically, the gangsters who will run the economy in all these regions will be linked to each other via the cash nexus. This is the new Enlightenment of globalism, which is not simply about inflows and outflows of capital.

The attempt to integrate the production, finance, and trade of the whole world under the authority of new "international" institutions (the Central Committee of the free-market fundamentalists) is the economic form taken to assert a new U.S. hegemony in the post-communist world. It has little to do with religion or identity or human rights. Economics is now concentrated politics. Much of the upheaval described by Juan Goytisolo are the "readjustments" needed to cement the new order.

The birth of political Islam filled a vacuum that came into

existence after the collapse of the international Left, but it is too archaic to have any lasting impact and it is worth remembering that the most hideous regime in the Islamic world—the Taliban creation in Afghanistan—is the direct product of U.S. policy.

Goytisolo's reflections make disturbing reading. They could not be further removed from the banal homilies on the plight of particular peoples that grace the Western media in times of crisis and are forgotten. The postmodern memory consists of glimpses and flashes. Goytisolo suggests that there are some things that should never be forgotten. Alas, there are too few of him left.

—Tariq Ali

SARAJEVO NOTEBOOK

THE CRACK MARKSMAN

The shortness of the path in no way diminishes the infinite span of the injustice   ANTONIO MACHADO

En route to the airport at Roissy via the Porte de la Chapelle, the publicity posters along the boulevard flash obsessively by the blackened manly face of an actor (Tom Berenger?) beneath capital letters of a film title: *SNIPER, CRACK MARKS-MAN*. The hero's crowning moment of glory pursues me left and right, from advertising hoardings and pillars, as if aiming a message at me personally. Is it a premonition, a sign, a sybilline warning? Or merely a god or seers' acknowledgment of the final destination of a journey that, according to my ticket, will be broken only in Rome and Split? I will never know, the taxi is already on the northbound carriageway, traversing the tunnel on the first ring road, leaving behind Paris and my final image of Paris: the true grit face of the Crack Marksman, the sublimated ideal and ineffable model of those shooting for real in Sarajevo.

Some two hours later I'm at one end of the passenger terminal in Fiumicino airport waiting for the Croatian Airlines departure. In the seats near the deserted check-in desk a flashily attired, self-absorbed group of travelers immediately captures my attention and triggers a worrying suspicion. I had read press reports that an Italian tourist agency was offering potential customers thirsting after strong sensations a special itinerary off the beaten track, in areas of the world recently devastated by war, where they might breathe the acrid smell of gunpowder, visit ruined villages and ghostly rooms emptied of their inhabitants, gaze from afar because of the stench—except those with the good sense to bring gas masks—at decomposed bodies, common graves lightly covered with earth, enormous piles of corpses. Surely the offer that initially encompassed Africa and Asia will have extended its range and reduced traveling costs the moment armed struggles and interethnic conflicts ceased to be a typically Third World speciality and took root on European soil. Only an hour from Rome, are the seekers after such singular encounters about to land on the Dalmatian coast and meet their peculiar guides? Perhaps these tourists fitted out in explorer gear—hats, binoculars, cameras, video cameras, knapsacks, shorts—are on their way to the land of Bosnia in their search for a succulent repast, a huge repertoire of genuine horror scenes, capable of satisfying the exquisite longings of the most demanding customers?

Is the group boarding with me to go to Split hoping to contemplate the corpse of the hunchbacked Adem, his spine miraculously straightened after being impaled on a stake by the doorway to his house? or the heads of the gypsy Ibro, his wife and son, stuck on posts in the fence around their house, "just as in the days of the Turk," according to Karadžić's men, for the mere crime of not running away? or the ashes of the disappeared Muslim village of Grapka, where all the inhabitants were burned after the atavistic ritual of mutilations, collective rape, and beheading in honor of the purifying god and invincible St. Sava? or to get a whiff opposite the Pósavina Hotel in Brcko of the last traces of the great orgy of blood and wine, when the sons of the *celestial fatherland* exterminated the *Turkish* population over three nights and four days, transported their corpses in freezers, then hurled them into the river Sava? or to train their binoculars on that unusual woman from Modrica, perched on the turret of a tank, waving her magic finger at the houses of her friends and neighbors so that a righteous mortar bomb would destroy them seconds later?* or to hunt for the traces of the unbelievable end of six pupils from the Vishegrad Institute for Handicapped Girls, executed, then thrown from the bridge into the Drina while other warring militiamen from the White Eagles hurled the rest into a minefield and practised

---

*These examples of the reign of barbarism in Bosnia have been gleaned from the moving testimony *Les Bosniaques* by Volivar Colic, a Bosnian writer exiled in France.

their renowned sharpshooting? or to take photos of women and children packed into deportation trucks after a punctilious cleansing operation, who died from dehydration in Prijedor, like the Jews of Treblinka? or the torched houses, carbonized bodies, demolished mosques of Vitez, Ahmici, or Donja Vecerska carried out by the forces of the Croatian Defense Council (HVO), their bravery vying with that of their Serbian rivals? or the Jasmin that Maite Rico spoke to whose arm was engraved with a cross and dagger by these new gallant knights in shining armor, like so many other hundreds of prisoners branded for ever with the four "Cs"—"S" in Cyrillic—, the acronym of the slogan *Samo Sloga Srbina Spasava*, that is, 'Only unity can save the Serbs," the favorite words of poet dreamer Karadžić and his valiant warriors? or the woman weeping in front of the TV camera, repeatedly raped by her upstairs neighbors in the "national" sector of Sarajevo and whose face was urinated on, while she was being raped, by the child of one of those patriots because her husband committed the unforgivable crime, deserted the *holy cause* to collaborate with "Islamic fundamentalists"? or perhaps they want to reconstruct the scene of the drama, recounted to Susan Sontag, of the Muslim wife of a Serb turned ultranationalist whose son was murdered in cold blood when the mother firmly said no and the lad resisted being dragged to the front hours before her exemplary enraged husband from Serbian balladry burst into their home and, without a single look of pity at his son's lifeless body, heroically executed his wife à la Calderón—public insults deserve public revenge—who was guilty of preventing him from doing his duty and thus of converting him into a despicably *tame* Serb?

Reality fortunately belies my apprehensions and, on our arrival at Split airport, I realize that the group probably comprises lovers of the natural beauties of the islands of Brac, Hvar, or Korcula, anxious to enjoy a few days' or weeks' holiday sunbathing and savoring the invigorating wine and delicious fish, pilgrims perhaps to that bare peak in Herzegovina where the Virgin regularly appears to the faithful and announces all manner of calamity and misfortune on the eve of the imminent apocalypse and definitive celestial victory.

For whatever reason, the fact is that tourists, albeit in small numbers, are returning to the Dalmatian coast and taking advantage of special packages on offers, thanks to the gradual emptying out of pensions and hostals temporarily occupied by fugitives from ethnic cleansing. Lying on the beach or by the edge of the swimming pools in their three-or-four-star hotels, can they be unaware of what is happening only a hundred kilometers away? Do they at least devote a fleeting thought to that diaspora of hundreds of thousands of people with nowhere to go, bombed by their former cocitizens or cruelly deprived of all way out or refuge? Isn't their saurian or reptilian indifference the same as greeted hungry exhausted Spanish Republicans in 1939 on the beaches of Argelès, herded behind barbed-wire fences? Did those French citizens who refused the defeated a jug of water and grimaced in horror as they spoke of the "reds" realise that the fascism victorious in the Peninsula would a year later take possession of their own land and that they would thus pay the consequences of the policy of nonintervention, their cynical folding of arms before the ravaged Republic?

My colleagues Alfonso Armada and Gervasio Sánchez, already accustomed to the bloody events and surreal happenings commonplace in the now defunct Yugoslavian Federation, take me to the hotel in Split where I stop to read various offers directed at journalists covering the news for the European and American press: "Self-Protection in Bosnia, Hire Your Own Security." A German bullet-proof car company offers a wide range of models, from an opulent Mercedes Benz 500 and Opel Senator to a humble Volkswagen! Pity the price list isn't included in the publicity.

Because of the late arrival of my flight from Rome I cannot travel with my friends. I have to wait until the day after to get my press card from the United Nations Protection Force (UNPROFOR) and leave on the French military plane that loads and unloads humanitarian aid on the shuttle to Sarajevo.

I use my free time to visit the walled remains of Diocle-tian's palace, stroll through the beautiful side streets of Trogir, climb one of the hills overlooking the bay of Split, and from there espy the islands of the Dalmatian coast, stretching out like crocodiles or hippopotami over the surface of the water, against the marine horizon.

On the way back to my hotel, I ask my taxi driver, with whom I communicate in Italian, where I could interview refugees from Bosnia-Herzegovina.

"In your hotel," he replies. "In the morning the nuns give them their food parcels,"

"To the Muslims as well?"

"This is a clean city. Their presence would scare off cus-tomers. We don't want them in Split."

"Where do you want them to go?"

"To Turkey or Libya. As far as I'm concerned, they can go to hell."

I shut my bedroom door and zap the remote till I get a Croatian news broadcast, devoted—what a delightful sur-prise!—to the daily activities, speeches, and audiences of genial President Tudjman. Can it be the hypnotic effect of the program or tiredness accumulated during the day? For the first time in years I fall asleep with the light on.

THE MOUSETRAP

The journey to Sarajevo has all the appearance of a game of blindman's buff that ends in a mousetrap. The French military Hercules that daily fly loads of humanitarian aid from Split to the Bosnian capital usually set aside a dozen side-seats for the press and for officials from international agencies and organizations. I realize on the airstrip at the Dalmatian airport that I am the only journalist: Sadako Ogata, director of the UN High Commission for Aid to Refugees (UNHCR) and her team of advisers occupy the remaining empty places. A swarm of photographers and cameras surround them as soon as we set foot on the ground, and soldiers hurriedly guide us through a labyrinth of corridors protected by walls and sandbags to an improvized press conference. An UNPROFOR armored car is to take me across the territory controlled by Serbian radicals to the former post office that is the start of the urban center still in the hands of the Bosnian presidency. Before that, I must sign a document in which I absolve the UNPROFOR forces of all responsibility for "loss, injury, or death" that may befall me during the journey. After what happened to Bosnian vice president Hakija Turajlić,who was quietly murdered while in one of these bullet-proof vehicles by Karadžić's militiamen, despite the presence of his escorts and their "violent protests" I can understand how the "blue berets" learned from their experience and now prefer to cover their own backs. The law of the survival of the fittest rules in Bosnia. The UN commanders' impotence, their resignation before the crimes and abuses of Karadžić and his cronies suggest an advertising slogan in keeping with the chancy nature of their transport operations: "You bring the corpse. UNPROFOR will see to the rest."

A Spanish NCO, forewarned by Alfonso Armada and Gervasio Sánchez, comes to meet me and helps me and my modest luggage into the armored car. The escort comprises Jordanian and Egyptian soldiers and, through a side peephole as we move forward I catch glimpses of a bleak, wasted landscape: houses with roofs blown off, blackened car chassis, truncated telephone posts, dead horses, roads plagued by potholes and leading nowhere.

In the post office car park, the game of blindman's buff is repeated: questioning, frisking, a brief labyrinth of sandbags, and finally we reach the hectic frontier building where French soldiers are offering their colleagues an exquisite cold buffet of canapés, chicken, meat, cakes, wine, and champagne on the occasion of the 14 July, *la fête nationale!* My friends find me in the office devoted to recording and archiving the data of press correspondents and we drive off at once in the direction of the Holiday Inn.

The Vojvode Putnika that runs across the modern part of Sarajevo has been renamed "Sniper Alley" by the besieged. In an illustrated guide to the capital published only seven years ago one can read this kind of description: "The city lights, like fireflies, punctuate the darkness more brilliantly than the stars of the Bosnian sky: this is the vista offered the tourist who reaches the outskirts of Sarajevo by night. If he journeys by day, he will discover an oriental city of the type that only exists in fairy tales and will be amazed to see broad avenues and brand new or nineteenth-century Austrian style buildings." But the city I now observe is but an area of devastation: wounded, mutilated, its guts hang out, its sores suppurate, its scars horrify. Entire streets and buildings have disappeared, no trams or buses circulate, the Vojvode Putnika is desperately empty, the trees have been felled, people crouch down in their hideouts. The facades of some ten- or twelve-story residential buildings present charred features or are covered in cavernous, yawning holes or disturbing eyelets. Reverberating glass skyscrapers rise up like hives of blind honeycombs: mirrors where the sun reflects and flashes alternate with empty eyesockets and wily one-eyed looks. Cars and buses reduced to ash prolong the horror of the conflagration in the middle of the roadway. Red and white trams, becalmed and bullet-ridden, gather rust by pavements invaded by weeds and wild shrubs. Trolley bus cables hang down dangerously between posts, curl around each other on the ground like snakes. There are buildings reduced to their metal frames, crushed and half-molten telephone booths and kiosks, useless, contorted wire fences, heap upon heap of scrap, vehicles disemboweled and black as coal. Almost no building has its windows intact: those that are still inhabited despite their exposure to the snipers have had their window space modestly covered with plastic patches supplied by UNPROFOR. In the midst of that geography of desolation a clock froze its hands at exactly eight o'clock (which day? which month? which year?). Without water, gas, electricity, public transport, or telephones Sarajevo looks at first sight like a phantom city, a dislocated skeleton or lifeless corpse. But the intermittent crackle of machine-gun fire, the occasional blast of mortars, the whistle of the snipers' bullets opportunely remind the visitor that its torture continues. In spite of the deluge of fire capriciously raining down and the cruel strangulation it is suffering, the Bosnian capital resists and miraculously remains on its feet.

As soon as a foreigner arrives in Sarajevo, he must familiarize himself with the laws and rules of an elementary code of survival. Accustomed to a free, untrammeled existence, his new space, the mousetrap shared with 380,000 human beings, forces a rapid apprenticeship on him: awareness of high-risk areas and of where one can move without excessive danger, of districts where the mortar bombs usually fall, of the snipers' favorite corners and paths, of places where it is better to walk with a stoop or which you must abandon at a moment's notice. Any distraction or miscalculation in the choice of route may prove fatal: as the people of Sarajevo tell you, anyone foraying into the open—and everybody has to go out in search of water, wood, or food—engages in Russian roulette. And so, as I find out on my first day, prudence advises departure from the hotel at full pelt, avoidance of Sniper Alley outside the former entrance to the Holiday Inn, then a scarper up the slope to the Kranjcevica, doubling back to reach the safer areas of Marshal Tito Avenue and the pedestrian zone of Vase Miskina. The cars that still circulate accelerate in a rush when they drive across an unprotected intersection, risking collision with another vehicle or one of the white UNPROFOR armored cars that tour the city throughout the day. To protect themselves from the "heroes" who lie in wait on neighboring hillsides and prefer to shoot at women and children, Bosnian army soldiers have blocked off the most dangerous gaps with whatever was at hand: containers, buses, cars, publicity hoardings that act as a curtain or screen against the bloodthirsty crusaders of Greater Serbia.

On the "safe streets," the people of Sarajevo stop to buy what they can or queue up at the fountains laden with water containers. But safety is an illusion and the ultranationalist Serbians are quick to dispel it the moment the population begins to drop its guard: the carnage opposite the bakery in Vase Miskina, on a young lads' sports ground, at the crowded fountains where water still spurts out, or on funeral cortèges in cemeteries, demonstrates that nobody, absolutely nobody can feel secure in any part of the city. A family from the block of houses near the hotel who fled their unprotected, windowless home at the beginning of a hailstorm of shells to hide in the bomb shelter died when it was blown apart by a mortar blast. Everyone runs the risk of bad luck or, if a believer, of the delicate touch of the wings of Azrael, the angel of death in Islamic religious tradition. In this city where there is no wood to make coffins, you must get used to sleeping, moving, walking about fully aware of your defenseless, precarious existence. Nobody can guarantee that a crack marksman hasn't chanced to get your insignificant self in his sights or that a grenade or shell won't explode inside your room.

The inhabitants of Sarajevo have withstood for more than a year this risk of extermination, their life as inmates of an open prison, with integrity, dignity, and sangfroid. But the combined effect of hunger, exhaustion, and a general feeling of betrayal and abandonment has finally overtaken them from the day the shameful Washington accord was signed, forcing their moral resistance to the limit of what is bearable. They have suddenly understood that the chips are down, that they must not expect help from any quarter: whether from white UNPROFOR armored cars that are unable to defend themselves or from the American planes that fly over the city on their futile, derisory mission to keep the airspace clean. In Sarajevo, as in the rest of Bosnia, murder, destruction, massacre—the whole infamous ritual known as ethnic cleansing—is conducted on the ground with impunity.

HOSPITALS, CEMETERIES,
OSLOBODENJE

The monthly news bulletin from the Health Ministry of the Bosnian presidency, published just before my arrival, starkly reveals the magnitude of the genocide perpetrated against the Bosnian people since April 1992: 140,000 killed (9,040 in Sarajevo), 151,000 wounded (53,095 in Sarajevo), 1,835,000 "displaced" people, 156,000 detainees in Serbian-Montenegran concentration camps, 12,100 paralysed and handicapped (1,280 children), and an approximate number of 38,000 women raped.

I've hardly settled in my hotel when I decided to visit the Kosovo hospital, the most modern and extensive in the city. The journey via Kranjcevica and Dure Djakovica is a first indication as to the deprivations and shortages of the beseiged: the majority of pedestrians are searching for water; they carry bundles of plastic containers or transport them in wheelbarrows, in trolleys of the kind you find in stations, airports and department stores, in prams, on bicycles, trucklebeds, skateboards, jugs carried aloft. The transport of wood also consumes the energies of several women and men who climb the hill in the district where the hospital stands.

The director of the orthopedic clinic, Dr. Faruk Kulenović, draws a somber picture of the situation: they've been nine days without water, without electricity, and only ten liters are left in the fuel tank that feeds the surgery generator. They are forced to operate in the daytime in the corridors most exposed to enemy fire, to take advantage of the light from the windows. They keep the generator for the injured who arrive at night.

"What would happen if today they threw thousands of grenades?"

"We would be forced to operate or amputate by candle-light or by oil lamp."

Dr. Kulenović takes me and my friends to a modern orthopedic unit sunk in darkness. The control panels, cardio-
graphs, and X-ray machine don't work for lack of electricity;
they urgently need anesthetics, bandages, antibiotics, and
syringes. The oxygen supply store is almost empty; the oper-
ating block is closed for the moment as the result of a shell
blast: as for the sterilizing unit in the rehabilitation center, it
is powered by firewood.

We visit the wards. On the stairs we pass mutilated patients
receiving therapy treatment: the one-armed, the lame with or
without crutches, a man without arms. In the ward with three
seriously wounded men, Dr. Kulenović points at a hole
opened up by a shell that passed between two beds and fortunately did not explode. Unbearable images of three recently
admitted women: two wounded by mortar bombs, the third
hit in the neck by a sniper's bullet when she was walking
along laden with containers on a search for water. Each case
is a story, each story an atrocity. Miroslav Bajic, forty-six years
of age, a Croatian, walks on crutches and sits on the edge of
his bed to talk. A grenade exploded right by him as he was
walking down the street and he bled for a long time, but
because of the bombing nobody could help him in the middle of the street. "The Chetniks, he says, want to sow hatred
in our hearts to prevent us from staying together. But look at
this ward: the beds are occupied by me, by a Serbian, and by
a Muslim. The three of us live here like brothers."

Three days later I return with my interpreter Alma to the
children's orthopedic unit in the same hospital. The person in
charge explains how his team of eleven doctors has operated
on 1,200 children since the start of the Serbian radicals'
aggression in conditions identical to those in the rest of the
hospital. At present they receive only one barrel of water a
day. In spite of the help from Medecins sans Frontières and
other humanitarian organizations, they are without practically
everything they need.

The post-op ward for children is a compendium and
showcase of the suffering imposed on the city. A little girl
with the stump of her leg in a bucket of water looks at me

distantly. Impossible to stop by her and ask her questions. The procession of wounded is a litany of pain: Azra, hit in the neck by a sniper two days before; Nazira, victim on 7 July of an incendiary grenade; Adis, hit two weeks ago cherry-picking with a friend; Almir, unable to keep up a smile, riddled by machine-gun fire nine days before near the airport and incommunicado with his family ever since; Elvedin, emaciated, skeletal, with the small eyes of a frightened animal. How can one explain such a high number of victims among the children? Is it possible that what the wounded Croat has just told me is true, that mercenaries and ultranationalists receive a double bonus for each woman, quintupled each time they score a hit on the diminutive target of a child?

The lack of an adequate diet is obvious from the thinness of patients. Where can they find the necessary milk, meat, and vitamin supplies if Karadžić's soldiers intercept the convoys of humanitarian aid, submit them to humiliating bargaining, and, despite promises and agreements, block their entry into Sarajevo for days on end? In the games room where a dozen children are recovering, drawing, or chatting around a table, the nurse sarcastically points out a big cuddly bear, a present, he says, from General Morillon.

On the hot days and nights there is a lack of space in the hospitals, a lack of space in the morgues—the corpses have to be lined up on the pavement—a lack of space in the cemeteries. Given that funerals were a favorite sniper target, others have had to be improvized in less exposed places (the park on the hill in Kovaci) or twilight hours have to be used to bury victims furtively (in the vicinity of the Olympic stadium built for the 1984 Winter Games). Their gravestones are quite unique: while the birthday of those laid to rest ranges over several decades, the date of passage is fixed, 1992 or 1993. The cause of death is well known and some of the victims have died in the cemetery. At the foot of the statue of the Lion, the marble slabs in the small civilian cemetery from the Tito era are now surrounded by memorials and stelas with crescent moons and five-pointed stars mixed up with Orthodox and Catholic crosses, also pointing toward the qibla. Death has

leveled and reunited the believers in the religions of the Book,
victims of the same barbarism. One should add to this com-
pacted harvest of funeral crosses and stelas another more
monumental memorial, with the dates of the 1948 UN
Universal Declaration on Human Rights, the 1950 European
Convention on Human Rights, the 1966 UN Agreement on
Civil and Political Rights, the 1990 Charter of the Paris
Conference on European Cooperation and Security, the
Founding Charter of the United Nations, and the renowned
Geneva Convention with the inscription "Here lie the dignity
of the European Community and the credibility of the United
Nations Organization perished in Sarajevo. They died from the
unrivalled cowardice and cynicism of their negotiators and
leaders," as a reminder to peoples throughout the world of the
worth of the moral commitment of the great powers—dozen
upon dozen of dishonored agreements and resolutions filed
away—when their vital interests are not at stake.

Perhaps the best example of the hatred of the pan-
Serbian fundamentalists and the courage of those who resist
them is the daily paper, now famous throughout the world,
Oslobodenje. The oval tower that once lodged the editorial
offices is now a mass disfigured by shellfire: a tortured,
Gaudian stalagmite structure or a begging, perhaps vengeful
stump. The insistent pounding of shells reveals the
besiegers' obsession with silencing the voice of the victims.
The day we go with Alma and Gervasio Sánchez, after driving swiftly along Sniper Alley, in the garden next to the front
of the building, protected against rifle fire, several journalists and print workers wash and hang out their clothes in the
sun or rest from their nocturnal labors in the shade of small
fir trees.

We enter the building almost in darkness. The print room
is in the basement and hasn't suffered from the shelling like
the rest of the building: beneath the two or three holes in the
ceiling, barrels with botched-up funnels catch rainwater and
stop it flooding the floor. The newspaper distribution room is
on the ground floor, in the area of the building less exposed
to ultranationalist bombs. As we go up to the first floor, the

spectacle is alarming: rubbish-filled corridors, devastated offices, ceilings that have caved in, filing cabinets torn apart, revolving chairs with their stuffing hanging out, heap after heap of broken panes of glass. We catch a glimpse of the front, 200 meters away, through cracks in the wooden protection shutters. The flag of the self-proclaimed Serbian Republic of Bosnia flutters on a nearby building. The zone between here and the skeleton of *Oslobodenje* is strewn with landmines. From May 1992, Karadžić's snipers have been shooting away but have not attempted to cross it.

In the cafeteria I talk to two of the journalists who, on seven-day shifts, ensure with forty-odd colleagues and print workers that the paper is printed and reaches the street. For security reasons, the editorial offices have moved to a flat off Marshall Tito Avenue, where, three days earlier, Alfonso Armada and ourselves interviewed its director Kemal Kurspahic and Zlatko Dizdarević, author of a "War Diary" published in France. The journalists tell me, "*Oslobodenje* in 1990 had 2,800 workers and published apart from the daily, eighteen cinema, sports, fashion, political and other magazines, distributed throughout Yugoslavia. The daily circulation was 70,000 and the total output reached a million copies. Now, because of lack of paper, we only print 3,000. Our stocks allow us to maintain this level for a maximum of a week. The newspaper sells out as soon as it goes on sale." According to the director, *Oslobodenje* urgently needs thirty liters of petrol: without that, the printing press cannot function. 30 August is their fiftieth anniversary and they can only reach that date with international support.

I've spent five days in the Holiday Inn and I still haven't seen the front facade. On the way back from our visit to the offices of *Oslobodenje,* we stop 300 meters away on Sniper Alley and, protected from the danger of a bullet by the battered building of the defunct Museum of the Revolution, I photograph the ugly yellow building, as solid as a luxury bunker, its welcoming flagstaffs stripped of their flags, and the awning or kepi flap over the entrance beneath which uniformed porters once used to greet guests as they alighted from their cars. Some shells have made inroads into windows and floors and given its nouveau riche pride quite a knock.

A strange home where, during my stay in Sarajevo, after interludes of deceptive calm, night and day I hear the whistle of bullets, the crackle of machine-gun fire, and the bangs from the mortars! I go to bed with two balls of wax in my ears under the constant impression that I am in a village in Andalusia or Castilla the day it is celebrating its patron saint.

THE RECORD OF THE HORROR

If we leaf through the statistics of the State Commission for Gathering Facts on the War Crimes in the Republic of Bosnia-Herzegovina, the figures speak for themselves: 650 eyewitnesses, 21,000 names of people murdered, 5,039 of war criminals, 169 concentration camps, 172 villages razed to the ground, 559 mosques destroyed.

These and other unimpeachable testimonies demonstrate the obvious desire of pan-Serbian fundamentalists—besotted by bloody mythology and an age-old longing to avenge the fourteenth-century defeat in the battle of Blackbird Fields in Kosovo—to exterminate the Bosnian Muslims in the strictly physical sense of the term. I won't rehearse the most shocking of these reports, but will just mention the one noted by David Rieff in his excellent account in the *New Yorker* from a conversation with José María Mendiluce, the former high-ranker in the UNHCR.

The episode took place in the small Bosnian city of Zvornik, at the time when it was being occupied by the notorious group of Serbian mercenaries known as the White Eagles. "I saw," Mendiluce affirms, "children placed under the wheels of tanks by fine, upstanding men and then crushed by other men in full possession of their faculties. These people have a coherent strategy. Their aim is to inflict the maximum terror on the civilian population, destroy the maximum property, and exercise the maximum violence on women and children. As soon as the mercenaries have accomplished their mission, the *established authorities*—the police of Karadžić's militia—arrive to *restore order.*"

The threats to create an international tribunal to try the crimes against humanity committed in the former Yugoslavia, given shape in numerous resolutions and agreements—the latest being the resolution of the 4 + 1 drawn up in Washington by Javier Solana—are, as Milošević, Karadžić, Mate Boban, and their ilk know too well, rhetorical exercises for the gallery, not worth the paper they're printed on. These criminals, known to everyone, travel to New York, Paris, London, and Geneva, are welcomed with smiles and full honors by the same men who issue "strong protests" in "harsh, unequivocal language" at the overwhelming mass of evidence of genocide and ethnic purification. This comedy enacted by both sides fools nobody. Radovan Karadžić, enveloped in the romantic glow of a poet who admires Walt Whitman, even pretends not to know the expression *ethnic cleansing,* which he stumbles over in response to journalists' questions, as if stunned by innocent surprise. Massacres, pogroms, death camps? An invention of the *mujaheddin,* the Islamic fundamentalists trying to dominate Europe! The habit of lying while knowing one is lying that H. M. Enzensberger spoke about in reference to intellectuals and apparatchik in the East, has been perfected in Belgrade and Pale, thanks to the "creativity and inventive imagination" in deceit raised to the height of an art in one of his novels by Dobrika Čosić, the defenestrated president of the Serbian-Montenegran Federation. The library in Sarajevo was burnt by the "Turks" of Alija Izetbegović to draw attention to themselves and accuse us of barbarism! The mosques blown to smithereens is the work of the *mujaheddin* attempting to mobilize world opinion against the Serbs! The recent attack that occurred as I write these lines on the UN fleet of vehicles in the district of Zetra, "a simple-minded scenario set up by the Muslims to sabotage the peace talks in Geneva and provoke a military intervention!" The butchery in the cemetery in Sarajevo, "a media ploy by the Bosnian Presidency to cover up Islamic expansionism"; as if Goebbels had described how the Jews in Auschwitz rushed into the gas chambers to win sympathy and stoke the fires of anti-Nazi propaganda. The target of almost universal, but empty, hypocritical rebuffs, Milošević, Karadžić, Šešelj present themselves as scapegoats in some Vatican-Islamic-Germanic plot. Only Russian nationalists, their Greek brothers, and the infallible protection of St. Sava can help them resist and guarantee the final victory of God's people of the ballads chanted in the midst of threatening intrigues!

Although the tactical agreement by the leaders of Serbia Great and Pure and Croatia Great and Pure to divide up the spoils of Bosnia-Herzegovina harasses the Bosnian Army and forces the Izetbegović loyalists to have recourse to methods employed by their enemies, the harshness of the conflict and fear of cleansing throw on the roads and byways in the Muslim controlled areas a terrified, hungry mass impossible to quantify: raw images of misery and pain at the heart of a thick-skinned, stonily selfish Europe, for which the disappearance of a sovereign state and the agony of a community of 2 million or so souls are just one more piece of news from the universe of sound and fury that Bush so far-sightedly styled "the new world order." Where will they go, these hundreds of thousands of refugees, harried on every side, the hapless object of abuse and violence? Ever since the joint Croat-Serb offensive, the territory of those faithful to the idea of a multiethnic State—now almost entirely Muslim—is reduced to less than 10 percent of their land and is still shrinking, without territorial continuity, like sharkskin. In spite of the tenacious resistance of its army, the map of Bosnia is being inexorably transformed into a set of human mousetraps, of beings packed into desperate conditions more precarious than those in Sarajevo.

On 17 July Alma drives me into the center of the city, to what in its day was the luxurious Europa Hotel, converted into a hostal for refugees after it was seriously damaged by bombing. In the desolate, bare lobby, without doors and windowless, several women sit chatting on the floor while young boys play football or hide and seek, running between the adjacent columns and ravaged terrace and park, where not a single tree survives. Sixty-five families, a total of 276 people, are living here, crammed in their rooms; refugees from the outskirts of Sarajevo, from Foca, Vishegrad, and Gorazde. We go up two flights of a banisterless staircase and enter a one-family room with settees, a mirror, and plastic chairs; Muslim rosaries hang on the wall alongside the Bosnia-Herzegovina coat-of-arms. The married couple Jasminka Butmic and Isak Crnogorcević give Alma a warm welcome and offer us all they have to offer: a bowl of rosewater. Both lived on the outskirts of Sarajevo up to the invasion of May 1992.

"The ultras act like programmed robots," she says. "No human feelings at all. They murder, pillage, and burn. Many of them are mercenaries from Russia and the Ukraine or criminals Milošević has released from Serbian prisons. They want to spread hatred among us, but they won't succeed. One day we'll live together again."

"Even after all the barbarity and bloodletting?"

"We won't forget, but we will forgive," he says. "There are Serbian families living here on the other side of the corridor. We help each other, we go down to the shelter together. Sarajevo has always been like that."

The general feeling of betrayal with regard to the UN and the European Union surfaces with bitterness.

"Of what use to us are security zones, American planes flying overhead, and the Blue Helmets in their armored cars if they keep on murdering us? We aren't afraid of an attack on the city. If they try, we can defend ourselves. That's how they want to starve us into surrender, by killing civilians with cowardly bullets."

We wait for a woman friend of the couple who is also a refugee in the hotel. When she doesn't appear, we decide to return to Jasminka and Ishak's room the following day.

The account by Abzija Meduserjac, a fifty-one-year-old widow, of what happened in Vishegrad in May 1992, deserves to be reproduced in full.

"The White Eagles stuck a butcher's hook down the throat of my neighbor, Ahmed Karishik. It was tied by rope to the back bumper of a car and they dragged him through the town so people could see him and hear his cries. Then they beheaded him and played football with his head. Finally they threw his remains into the river.

"They hacked the arms off another acquaintance, Hasan Brko, and forced him to drink his own blood. He was also beheaded and thrown in the river.

"The White Eagles came from Vukovar, but they recruited a lot of Serbs in the town. A neighbor brought them to our house. They asked after my eldest son, enlisted in the Bosnian army, then said they would be back. I was afraid for my daughter, and sent her to another part of the town where she could hide and save her life. At ten P.M. the following night they came without the neighbor. They beat me and my younger son, forced us to lie on the floor by aiming their revolvers at us, and forced me to put the barrel of a loaded pistol in my son's mouth while I was kicked and pummeled trying to get the gun to fire. Suddenly they tired of their game, and, for some reason, left us alone. I was speechless for eight days: I couldn't make a single sound.

"The Muslims who took refuge in Gorazde were promised they could return safely. The people who believed that perished. They forced more than 300 inside the Old Mosque, near the bus station, and set it on fire. I'll never forget their cries of terror and the smell of burnt flesh.

"There were girls who tried to commit suicide by throwing themselves out of the rooms where the White Eagles locked them up in order to rape them later. A neighbor and her seventeen-year-old daughter were raped, beheaded, and thrown in the river. One girl managed to escape from a house they doused in petrol and set alight, no skin, no hair, scorched, a living sore, like a ghost or skeleton. She was saved and is in a hospital in Ljubljana. 'I live,' she said, 'in order to bear witness.' "

"Did the Serbs in the town collaborate in these brutalities?"

"A lot did. It seems incredible but it's true. But a minority did stand aside and even tried to help us."

"Do you think you could live with them again?"

Abzija's face darkens, her eyes seem to stare into space.

"I don't know. It would be very difficult for me to live alongside the man who gave us away."

MEMORICIDE

"You must walk this city patiently," I read in a guide to Sarajevo published a few years ago, "if you want to discover it, find the main districts and understand how its heart always beats in old Carsija, the popular area of bazaars, traders, bystanders, and tourists. You must visit Bascarsija, the present name for this part of town, on foot. The few car parks on its periphery are difficult to locate."

From the second day of my stay I have followed this advice and taken advantage of the gaps in my daily schedule, preferably at the time of day when the guns go quiet and a deceptive feeling of peace reigns over the besieged capital.

In photos, the main triangular-shaped plaza descending the slope from the start of Marshal Tito Avenue to the small mosque in Bascarsija seems brimming over with life and energy. Today it is a deserted space exposed to mortar blasts and shells from the pan-Serbian extremists stationed on the hills the other side of the river. Various rusty street stalls stand battered and empty, a miserable advertising column displays tattered posters for defunct cultural activities, a yellow lorry has been immobilized forever next to a beautiful Ottoman wooden kiosk with a striated dome that is topped by two balls and a tiny crescent. The bazaars are barred over or have been gutted by shellfire, their reddish roofs holed or scarred by direct hits, the useless traffic lights and markers of a tourist route are a derisory reminder of happier times gone by.

All the intersecting streets that lead to Vase Miskina contain similar lines of empty bazaars, pavements with deserted awnings, Spanish-style tiles advertising a barber's, or an eye-catching Grill Dôme. The Brusa covered market has been closed down, but around the equally shut main city mosque I spot faint signs of life: a few goldsmiths; a hairdresser; two bookshops selling Muslim religious works, one window with a translation of *Europe and Islam* by the excellent Tunisian historian Hichem Djait.

The beautiful mosque of Gazi Husref Bey built in 1531—
one of the masterpieces of Ottoman-Balkan architecture—
has received a total of eighty-six mortar blasts, but both the
body of the building and its delicate minaret still survive. The
interior was badly damaged and is being restored. The marble stairs to the pulpit stand out alone and miraculously
unscathed between the scaffolding and plastic sheeting over
the *mihrab* and the *maqsura*.

The most desolate spectacle is the ancient Institute for
Oriental Studies, the famous Library of Sarajevo. On 26
August 1992, Serbian ultranationalists rained down a host of
incendiary rockets that reduced the entirety of its rich cultural
heritage to ashes in a few hours. As the press office of the
government of Bosnia-Herzegovina points out, this act "constitutes the most barbarous attack on European culture since
the Second World War." The fact is that the band of mediocre
novelists, poets, and historians with a vocation as arsonists,
whose report to the Belgrade Academy was the seed of
Milošević's rise to power and the subsequent breakup of
Yugoslavia—the crime cannot be properly described except
as *memoricide*. Since every trace of Islam must be removed
from the territory of Greater Serbia, the Library, the collective
memory of the Bosnian Muslim people, was condemned a
priori to disappear in the avenging, purifying flames.

Almost five centuries after the burning of the Arab manuscripts by the Bibarrambla Gate to Granada decreed by
Cardinal Cisneros, the episode has been repeated on a larger
scale during the Fifth Centenary Commemorations. Determined to right the wrongs in the history of their country, the
forgers of Serbian national mythology—so eloquently
denounced by compatriots of the standing of Djuric and
Bogdanovic—fulfilled their ancestral dreams of annihilation:
thousands of Arab, Turkish, and Persian manuscripts disappeared forever. The treasure thus destroyed comprised works
of history, geography, and travel; theology, philosophy, and
Sufism; natural sciences, astrology, and mathematics; diction-
aries, grammars, and anthologies of poetry; treatises on music
and chess. Today all that remains of the library is the hollow

frame of its four facades adorned by columns, horseshoe arches, rose windows, and turrets. The metal structure of the roof through which the rockets fell looks like an enormous spider's web, the pillars of the inner courtyard preserve little of the delicate stucco work, the central area is a huge pile of rubbish, debris, beams, and charred paper. I pick a piece up, see it is a catalog card from the archive, and take it with me as a souvenir of this programmed barbarism, the purpose of which was to sweep away the historic substance of a land and mount in its place an edifice made of lies, legend, and willful amnesia.

If the Komites, Hayduks, and Chetniks were never punished for their assaults on Muslims in the last two centuries, why should they be punished now by a European Union that is falling apart, victim of the contradictions, small-mindedness, and egoism of its own architects? On the new map of the Balkans, drawn in blood and fire by the defenders of the primacy of national, religious values, the mere name of Sarajevo symbolizes the existence of a cosmopolitanism that is hated and seen as an affront: a space for encounters and convergence, a point where differences rather than being a reason for exclusion mingle and cross-fertilize through osmosis and permeability. The Bosnian capital embodies—I find it difficult to write embodied—a distinct, stimulating, open concept of a European city. Blind, deaf, and dumb, we are allowing it to be destroyed.

One only has to cross the trickle of the Milyacka River by the bridge near the library to be in the heart of the left bank coveted by the "Serbian Republic of Bosnia," the small Jewish community gathered around the synagogue. There is a long queue of people in the street overlooked by its pink, ochre facade, large windows, rosaces, and domes capped by the six-pointed star: they are customers of the "Hebrew chemists," the best stocked in the city. In the building next to the temple—where there have been no services for some time through lack of a rabbi—a charity organization whose name—*La Benevolensia*—has a clear Spanish ring, daily distributes hundreds of bowls of soup to the starving population. To reach the first floor you have to make your way through the mass of Sarajevans who come to fill their stomachs or communicate with their families who have fled to Croatia or are resident in areas loyal to the Bosnian presidency via a small radio station set up in one of the rooms.

David Kamhi, vice president of the Jewish Humanitarian, Cultural and Educational Society is a violinist and looks just like a member of a Spanish provincial casino: bald-headed, lively, bespectacled, like those sitting among the smoke and noise of their countrymen opposite a stack of cards or a domino board. His Spanish—"not *ladino* but Jewish-Spanish"—he points out—is amazingly rich and modern. David Kamhi is a descendent of the Jews expelled from the Peninsula in 1492 who spread through the lands of the Ottoman Empire and settled in Sarajevo in 1551.

"'Before the Nazis arrived there were 14,000 of us, 10,000 Sephardic Jews. Most died when deported. Of those who escaped some remained hidden in the city, others came back at the end of the war.

"In April 1992, the community had 1,400 members, mainly Sephardic as I am. When religious restrictions came to an end with the death of Tito, many people discovered their Jewish roots and moved close to us. There were 700 in the autumn of last year when the siege was established. Now there are about as many of us who have refused to leave.

"Since Bosnia became independent," he lamented, "not a single diplomat from your country has visited us. Why don't you send a representative to Sarajevo? Perhaps we don't exist? I am Bosnian, I am Jewish and I am Spanish. Many of my colleagues are called Pardo, Pinto, Alcalay, Alfandari, Mercado. My first language was Spanish. I've created an association of Bosnian-Spanish Friendship, I was in Madrid on the occasion of the Fifth Centenary and shook hands with King Juan Carlos.

"It is shameful that Spain ignores us and doesn't maintain relations with Bosnia. The only people who visit and help us are army officers and commanders. General Delimiro Prado was here chatting in this office. I heard that the king offered the Spanish passport to all Sephardim. But how can that work out, if you don't open a consulate here?

"In Bosnia there were very good relations between the religious communities. They used to call Sarajevo Little Jerusalem. Muslim lads worked and learned their trade in our workshops. Sarajevo is a mixture: multicultural, multiconfessional, and multinational. In this neighborhood of Sarajevo, the synagogue is a few steps from the mosque, which is a few steps from the Catholic and Orthodox Churches. Now we have been put in a ghetto, in a concentration camp of 380,000 people. It's unbelievable that Europe should allow this after the Nazi genocide!

"Humanitarian aid? That's a joke! We don't receive a fifth of what we need: only humiliating alms. I'll be blunt: they're sending us stocks of food and clothes they couldn't sell. The savages up there shoot at us indiscriminately: they kill us because we live together and want to go on living together. The idea of an Islamic threat in one of Milošević's lies. He and his gang are the real fanatics."

Like all Sarajevans, David Kamhi prefers not to think about the future: the burden of the present is already too great and there is no possible way out.

"We Jews don't even have anywhere to be buried"—is his parting comment—"our cemetery is on the front line. The Chetniks dug their trenches there and profaned it."

ONE WAY TO EARN A LIVING

The hotels that open their doors to the press in the centers of conflict on the planet are often endowed with a romantic, dreamy aura as a necessary counterpoint to the stress and difficulties of the daily labors of the chroniclers, photographers, and television teams: the aristocratic serenity of the American Colony Hotel in East Jerusalem, with its beautiful patio, microclimate, and leisure areas is a real oasis of calm after the tense hours, plagued with violent incident, devoted to filming the *intifada*. The shape and structure of the Holiday Inn in Sarajevo are the kiss of death to any such romantic temptation: the huge entrance hall is in fact a central patio twelve or thirteen floors high under a ceiling dotted with skylights. The initial impression of a religious temple fades with the vista of the three big concrete supporting pillars, and the central minibar covered with a kind of striped parasol shaped like a Polynesian beach hut or an extravagant green-red-and-yellow-striped sombrero, imported directly from Disneyland. The boarded-up side door, windows cracked or covered in UNPROFOR plastic sheeting, the small ladder forever leaning against the wall are worrying symptoms of an abnormal situation. Signs to the International Restaurant, Bosnian Restaurant, Herzegovinan Restaurant, Nightclub, Casino, Duty Free Shop, Exchange, Cafeteria, evoke infinitely remote days of prosperity. The present one and only dining hall tucked away on the mezzanine is the old conference room. At dawn, the battered, livid Holiday Inn, its floors looking over the entrance hall like galleries and cells in a large prison, is like a metaphor for the city, a luxury prison implanted in the midst of a vast concentration camp of open-category prisoners, the inhabitants of Sarajevo who queue patiently with their containers waiting for the water supply lorry at the only corner of the hotel protected from snipers. Only at night when the electric light goes, does the flickering light of candles and pocket lamps—like nocturnal emblems of smugglers or *carabineri*—create a more striking, pleasant illusion of a modernist crypt erected in honor of some superior abstract bearer of justice.

At the end of the afternoon, its purple seats, with their vaguely spiderly presence, not only support the weight of journalists and members of the humanitarian aid associations—the hotels' only customers—but also that of their assistants and interpreters, and a select group of young and not-so-young Bosnians able to pay dollars or marks for a beer or drink. In spite of the frequent roundups of civilians fit to hold a gun like the one carried out there weeks before—and in the few open cafés and bars in the city—by the men of Musan "Caco" Topalović, one of the most radical, turbulent commanders in the Bosnian army, the deserters and refugees from the front have begun to reappear discreetly in the areas of the entrance hall served by the minibar.

The war—and generally all extreme situations—show up as on a photographic negative the moral character and secret identity of those living through it: their cowardice or courage, rectitude or lack of scruples, selflessness or egoism. Sarajevo is a microcosm where everyone shows their true colors in their daily behavior and activity. The unhappiness and misery of some—the immense majority—benefits and enriches others. While ill-equipped and hungry in trenches on Mount Igman or the Žuć hills hundreds of young Bosnians suffer the devastating hammer blows of Karadžić's shells, others frequent places where you can only pay in foreign currency and amass fortunes on the black market.

A visit to the city center during one of the pauses in the Serbian artillery fire is particularly instructive. Hundreds of nervy or exhausted people hunting all manner of products pile into the covered market, around the stalls and the huddled groups buying and selling on Marshal Tito Avenue. Along the pavement, black marketeers or their straw men offer soap, toothpaste, tinned food, chocolate, various brands of cigarettes to passersby. A little further on, other pedestrians are consulting proposed swaps stuck on the wall or the obituaries and photographs of the deceased.

Accompanied by Alma, I venture into the market and find out the price of what is on sale: a packet of biscuits, 10 marks; a box of Marlboro, 12; three radio batteries, 15; a kilo of sugar, 40; a liter of oil, the same; a kilo of flour, 10. If one takes into account that a hospital doctor earns 10 marks a month, that the average salary varies between 3 and 5, and that pensioners from Tito's army or partisans only make 2, the question springs to mind—where the hell do these people get their money? and brings with it the obvious response: if all Sarajevans are suffering the consequences of the siege, a minority is suffering less than the rest.

There is an identical panorama at the front of the market; bundles of wood, tinned zucchini, razor blades. Some people are selling greens, cabbages, spindly carrots grown in their gardens or domestic patches in rooms disemboweled by artillery or in useless bathtubs. Others, small pears, cherries, and raspberries picked in their gardens. As in the covered market, there are plenty of tins of roast beef and other treasures sporting the emblem of the European Union, the result of humanitarian aid.

Just over a year ago, *Oslobodenje* journalist Zlatko Dizdarević wrote in his *Sarajevo: A War Journal**: "The French and the Canadians arrived at Sarajevo airport today to ensure the safe delivery of canned goods to black marketeers. Whatever they don't want is then distributed to honest folk." The truth that shocked more than the odd person at the time is now common knowledge, out in the open: some members of UNPRO-FOR are getting rich on this lucrative trade and are singled out in local gossip. Welcomed as saviors on their arrival, one year later they are the object of unconcealed contempt and hatred. Dizdarević writes: "Is international public opinion aware of the price out of town in one of the UNPROFOR's vehicles? Sarajevans certainly are. It is one hundred German marks, cash, counted out into a Blue Helmet's hand."

The brutality of the siege and the tensions it creates has

---

*Zlatko Dizdarević. *Sarajevo: A War Journal*. Translated by Anselm Hollo. New York: Fromm International, 1993.

forced a good number of the besieged, especially Croats and Serbs, to seek salvation in flight. According to figures from the Bosnian presidency, 1,300 or so people with family resident abroad have official permission to leave, but UNPRO-FOR forces refused to take responsibility for the protection of the convoy of refugees through areas under Karadžić's control for fear of extortion and pillaging by his men, the pretext being (you may well laugh!) that they didn't want to contribute indirectly to the ethnic cleansing. While the traditional atmosphere of multicultural coexistence, the pride of the Sarajevans, gradually but irremediably deteriorates, the number of people waiting to escape from the siege grows daily. The disappearance of a well-known surgeon of Serbian stock from the orthopedic clinic at Koševo hospital—the talk of the war correspondents during my stay in the city—was carried out, according to general opinion—via UNPROFOR cars.

Information collected by my colleagues records how groups of radical militiamen and uncontrolled bands of refugees from other areas whose homes and families were burned and decimated by the ultranationalists are harassing citizens with Serbian forebears and dragging them into the front lines. The hesitant words of the woman witness to the horrors and killing in Vishegrad about possible future coexistence with the criminals and their accomplices reflects a minority position but one with a tendency to grow and win support. "If there is no way out, people become dangerous, everyone fights for his own life, loses respect for everyone else and becomes an animal," a soldier from the Bosnian army who was mutilated by the explosion of a grenade remarked in my presence when being interviewed by Alfonso Armada. The death toll in the siege imposed by the pan-Serbian fundamentalists and the daily realization of betrayal and abandon by the UN and the European Union undermines the cosmopolitan spirit of tolerance typical of Sarajevo. The heroic defense on the part of the Bosnian presidency and the Muslims and others loyal to Alija Izetbegović of a common citizenship against the homogenizing, tribal conceptions of their Croat and Serbian ultranationalist adversaries is constantly losing ground as the siege tightens and despair spreads. The psychological tension of the 380,000 people caught in the mousetrap grows by the day and crystallizes in a feeling of anger and frustration toward UNPROFOR.

The decision to send humanitarian aid to the terrorized and starving towns has clearly saved many lives. The presence of the blue berets has certainly prevented the carrying out of further bloody and odious massacres. But that Good Samaritan role of ill-armed forces continually exposed them to the aggression and blackmail of Karadžić's ultras, turned them first into spectators and then into mute accomplices of the aggressors. UNPROFOR has never prevented—because of the strict mission they were assigned—the martyrdom of Sarajevo nor of the other "security zones" established on paper in the mockery of the Washington agreement. Worse still, the permanent presence of the blue berets has acted as a sound argument for the supporters of military nonintervention and enemies of lifting the arms embargo, which so cruelly punishes the victims. Any violent action, they maintain, would endanger the lives of UNPROFOR soldiers and officials of the UN High Commission for Refugees (UNHCR). International humanitarian aid is thus brandished as a weapon to veto the besieged citizens of Sarajevo's legitimate right to self-defense. Meanwhile, in violation of all international law, Clinton fires his rockets at Iraq while invoking article 51 of the United Nations Charter and that act is received with "understanding" by Western chancelleries, the very same chancelleries that obstinately deny Bosnian Muslims recourse to the same article—the right to legitimate self defense that would at least permit them, as they say, 'to die with dignity." To argue that the sending of arms to save a country under attack would be a futile prolongation of the war and the suffering of the peoples involved should make Lord Owen, the honorable European Union negotiator, blush with shame: without President Roosevelt's massive supply of arms to Great Britain, the war could in effect have been concluded in 1941 with a Hitlerian peace just like the peace now being drawn up with Serbian war criminals. Did

Churchill's refusal to accept the "new realities" created on the map merely prolong the war and suffering of the peoples of Europe? Or did it not perhaps save them from the unbearable yoke of barbarism?

Western political double standards, already made manifest in Kuwait and Palestine, has once more been cruelly exposed in the defunct Yugoslavia: the thirty-seven resolutions and thirty declarations of the UN Security Council relating to Serbian aggression have gone straight into the wastepaper basket. "Security zones" bombed daily without riposte, humanitarian aid paying tolls or cut off by Karadžić's warriors! Snipers posted on buildings and hills adjacent to Sarajevo who shoot and will go on shooting at women and children with total impunity! Will anyone move a finger to stop this scrupulous cleansing operation? The arena for these exploits does not figure in the zones of "vital interest" to the United States or the European Union. A Bosnian is worth less than a barrel of crude. Muslims and others loyal to the Sarajevo government expiate their only crime, that of belonging to a country without oil wells.

AN ORTHODOX ARC FOR THE
ISLAMIC SERPENT

Last June, Monsignor Seraphim, the primate of the Greek Orthodox Church, officiated at a special mass in Athens replete with political-religious homilies and sermons in support of Radovan Karadžić's Serbian ultranationalists. All the parties of the right and the left and the Greek trades union organizations were on the platform. Inflammatory orators castigated "Muslim expansionism in the Balkans." How can we stop it? "We must forge an arc of orthodoxy against the Islamic snake," bellowed one prelate. In other words: imitate the Chetniks, the vanguard of Christianity.

Right from the start of their aggression against Bosnia, Serbian radicals have raised, both inside and outside their country the specter of the "fundamentalist" threat orchestrated in the shadows from Tehran. Their war thus took on a religious fervor aimed at coloring their homogenizing, irredentist plans with the hues of the secular struggle in Europe against the Muslims and their attempt to create a "Caliphate in the Balkans" with the support of the "Turkish fifth column" that has infiltrated Germany—the almost 2 million immigrant workers. These fantastic lucubrations, repeated day and night for years by Milošević's television, have sunk into the minds of many Serbs—and now Greeks—till they have been convinced they are legitimately defending themselves against the supposed genocide planned by the *mujaheddin*.

> For five centuries, Serbs
> have suffered slavery
> glorifying the name of St. Sava.
> St. Sava loves Serbians
> and intercedes with God for them.
> Sing, Serbs
> Now sing this song three times!

Television propaganda from Belgrade and Pale, caught by satellite disk on the Dalmatian coast, carries images of an unforgettable lyrical candor: a blond, healthy girl, decked out in traditional Serbian costume and surprisingly similar to the young Valkyries on Hitler's mass processions, bows graciously to kiss the mortar that disgorges its grenades on the "Turks" of Sarajevo. In a tryptich of warning to our European "friends," the first figure shows the fluttering EU flag; the second, the same flag splashed with runny green lines; the third a totally green flag and a caption bleating: "This is the future." Green, naturally, represents Islam and the message from Milošević and Karadžić—reiterated by Franjo Tudjman, as clumsy and belated as ever—is more than transparent: their soldiers are fighting to defend Europeans against the *flood tide* of infidel invasion. Serbian nationalist mythology has resurrected the glorious epoch of the Crusades: the day of my departure General Ratko Mladić, leader of Karadžić's ultras, had this comment to make as he launched the offensive against the last defenses of the Bosnian loyalists on Mounts Bjelasnica and Igman: "From now on my army controls the way of Allah." The final victory of the paladins of racial purity, ratified as I write these lines by the breakup of Bosnia-Herzegovina and its replacement by a chimerical Federation of Bosnian Republics established along ethnic lines, must have overjoyed Jean-Marie Le Pen—whose acolytes, according to a key report by the *National Geographic* correspondent—maintain regular contact with Karadžić in Pale—strengthening him in his vision of a France without immigrants, a French France in line with the model of a Serbia Great and Pure.

"In the eyes of many Europeans, even the most open, liberal, lay Muslims are fundamentalists." The man uttering these words in his office on the first floor of the Gazi Husref Islamic School is Mustafa Ceric, the *rais* or president of the imams of Bosnia. His black tunic, slightly greying beard, and immaculate white cap with its thin red border around his forehead confer on him an air of great nobility and dignity, like a figure in an Ottoman painting who has stepped out of the canvas and suddenly come to life. He's been talking to me for more than half an hour without an interpreter in excellent English with a smattering of Arabic. He spontaneously sketches the broad lines of his biography: he studied theology and religious sciences in the Al Azhar university in Cairo, and was imam for the last decade in the main mosque in Chicago.

"I am the only member of the Muslim religious community in Bosnia educated both in the Near East and the West. Until last year I firmly believed in the humanist values of Europe: its democratic ideals, the Universal Declaration of Human Rights, the freedom of belief at the heart of its lay states, that is, in the noble precepts inscribed in their constitutions. The Bosnian people—Muslims and many Croats and Serbs— believed in them as well: they wanted to live within the framework of a multiethnic, multicultural state. Since May 1992 we have been sacrificing our lives for the principles of the United Nations Charter. And what has happened? Instead of helping us, European governments, led by England and France, have folded their arms: they are allowing us to be exterminated and deny us the right to defend ourselves by imposing an arms embargo that leaves us defenseless at the mercy of the enormous arsenal of the Yugoslavian army that Milošević confiscated for his own personal use.

"After this bitter cup, I can no longer believe in European humanism. The ideas worthy of respect in the Universal Declaration on Human Rights have died in Bosnia. Tens of thousands of men and women who also supported them are now stacked up on top of each other through lack of space in the cemeteries of Sarajevo or lie in common graves throughout the territory of Bosnia. Say it loud and clear: they died defending these ideas in the midst of the indifference or hypocritical compassion of European statesmen and diplomats.

"The West will no longer be able to give us moral lectures: it has allowed the architects of ethnic cleansing, an imitation of the Nazi model, to rape and systematically murder women and children, create concentration camps, and reduce our past to ashes with absolute impunity. You who are very proud that you defeated Fascism, don't you realise how it has risen again and is burning down the inside of your own house? Have you become blind and deaf to the barbarism destroying Sarajevo?

"On the one hand, you talk of punishing the guilty of crimes against humanity, and on the other you conduct friendly dialogues with them and endorse their conquests. We the victims are the ones who have been punished: left defenseless, bombed, starving, our medical aid blockaded. The initial responsibility for this tragedy falls on Milošević, Karadžić and the fanatical supporters of Greater Serbia, but that of the European Union is no less great. Its governments have refused to put their principles into practice, they have behaved cynically and scornfully toward the weak."

"What about the humanitarian aid?"

"What use is drip-feeding if they allow them to cut our heads off?"

"Invoking the fundamentalist threat is not an exclusively Serbian practice. More than one Western politician has developed a strategy along these lines."

"That's the heart of the problem. Many Europeans are locked in the formula of the historic confrontation of Christianity with Islam. The specters from the past weigh like a nightmare on their subconscious. The Chetniks use that, whip up atavistic frenzies, perpetuate the crusading spirit, and proclaim themselves as championing Europe against the 'Turks.' This would be laughable if it weren't a question of life and death for us.

"The West thinks it possesses the monopoly of truth, morality, and right behavior but in reality it wants to maintain its political and economic domination over Muslim peoples and, generally, those it calls Third World; it uses every means to stop us uniting; it tries to make us believe we are incapable of resolving our problems without its advice or help. It is perfectly aware of its technological, economic, and military superiority, but fears our spiritual strength because it knows that it has none."

I ask him about the plan for ethnic partition, for a federation or confederation of states, discussed by the UN and EU negotiators.

"Lord Owen has no honor or shame. He has treated us to a string of lies and unkept promises followed by threats and bribes to make us yield to force and accept what he calls new realities. He has never considered Bosnia to be a sovereign state. He is the true figure of a man without principles, unable to distinguish criminal from victim who, in the end, becomes an active accomplice in the crime."

The conversation drifts into more personal areas: the psychological consequences of the terror and siege. Does he think himself personally capable of preserving the humanism that he invokes, of resisting the maelstrom of ethnic hatred?

"It's a difficult situation," Mustafa Ceric concedes. "The Chetniks are systematically propagating racial confrontation, want to extinguish any embers of *merhimet* (forgiveness and pity) in our hearts. They consider this feeling, our repugnance at following their methods, as proof of our meekness and inferiority. Consequently, though we must never give up on that attitude, we must become warlike and strong, stop them from annihilating or dispersing us like the Palestinians. They want to extirpate Islam from the Balkans. The time has come for us to abandon dead ideals and preserve the existence and faith of our community."

In the late afternoon, as I transfer the notes of my interview to the pages of my notebook, the sniper fire intensifies. Susan Sontag arrived some hours ago and I dine with her, David Rieff, and the photographer Annie Leibovitz in the hotel dining room. Although it is Monday and we can't avail ourselves of the modest self-service buffet, our "entertainer" for the evening is playing some sentimental, vaguely familiar tunes on the piano. The Holiday Inn is in darkness: we converse by candlelight. There is a loud background noise of shelling and machine-gun fire; the atmosphere is surreal. Someone hands me the bulletin from the Institute for Public Health: in the last thirty-six hours artillery fire and sniper bullets have killed eight and wounded thirty-five!

The soirée goes on longer than usual, and as I leave our

table, holding my flashlight, I note that our "entertainer" has slipped off safe and sound,

Nobody shot the pianist!

EUROPE'S SHAME

"Let us consider the poor image these democracies—once the pride of the world—now project of themselves," wrote Antonio Machado in 1938, commenting on their desertion of the Spanish Republic: "let us see what they concoct in their chancelleries, now unable to invoke even a protocol expression of dignity, a single ideal principle, a single strict norm of justice. As if they had been defeated in advance, or surreptitiously sold off to the enemy, as if they sensed the key to the future was no longer in their grasp. . . . Let us consider the miserable performance of the League of Nations, which is transforming a most noble institution, that should have honored the whole of humanity, into a superfluous if not pathetic body, which would make it a laughing-stock if it did not coincide with the most tragic moments in contemporary history."

Can one imagine a more up-to-date, on-target description of that theater of Chinese shadows, of the contradictory declarations from Clinton, the eternal debates in the UN Security Council and among European Union leaders aimed at gradually leading the Bosnian president Alija Izetbegović to unconditional surrender, like the bull the matador has just run through, which his team now brings skillfully to its knees so he may end its days with one clean, clinical jab. We all know the name of the matador has his team, those picadores and banderilleros disguised as "negotiators," for whom punishing the aggressor would be "impolitic," since in Bosnia "they have all sinned and no side is free of guilt' (except of course, the picador-in-chief, model of decency and rectitude, whose greatness will live on forever!).

Has the history of Europe in the 1990s been a mere repetition with slight symphonic variations, of the obfuscation and absurdities of the 1930s (Austria, Ethiopia, Spain, Czechoslovakia)? a dreary, interminable Ravel's *Bolero*?

I agree with the Spanish ambassador to the United Nations when he admits that if initial responsibility for the tragedy rests with the Serbian leaders, the international community has shown its absolute impotence when it comes to heading it off. A decisive reaction to Milošević's racist, expansionist program could have crushed in the bud this disturbing resurrection of the past. His determination to destroy the Yugoslav Federation and substitute one totally dominated by Serbia would inevitably lead to its implosion and a generalized war. Europe's silence at the brutal repression unleashed in Kosovo and the abolition of its statute of autonomy was Milošević's first test of the selfish indifference of the EU governments. When this test was breezily passed, his ambition and appetite increased. The transformation of the federal army into a Serbo-Montenegrin army spelled breakpoint in a process that the European Union could still have interrupted. Everything had been planned and planned well: in September 1991, Ante Marković, then prime minister of the Federation, revealed the existence of an intrigue between Milošević and the army leaders, aimed at uniting all the Serbian peoples scattered throughout Yugoslavia into a single homogeneous state. In later statements to the newspaper *Vreme*, Marković divulged a recording of conversations between the Serbian prime minister and Radovan Karadžić, in which the ultra leader revealed his role as a humble agent of his master in Belgrade: their division of labor, respectively playing the hawk and the dove to public opinion—a game later pursued by Karadžić and his right-hand man, General Ratko Mladić—is part of the script that was written then and the politicians and observers who believed the genuine nature of their divergences were deluded just as Chamberlain and Lord Runciman were when they trusted the word of Hitler and the leader of the Sudetens. In his dual, ever reversible role as good guy and bad guy, the unrivaled model poet and psychiatrist now asserts with dovelike innocence that both he and his comrade Boban are prepared to offer the Muslims a *quality space* where they can create their own State or *yamahrîa*, leaving the leader of the self-proclaimed Serbian Parliament of Bosnia the responsibility of affirming— this time for real: "Sarajevo will be ours." Only Lord Owen,

Hurd, and their European colleagues seem to take this game seriously. Will this quality space with green areas and "land rich in resources" promised key in hand to the defeated be an idyllic Swiss canton in Karadžić's lyric mode or a site for the final Palestinisation of Bosnian Muslims, trapped and dispersed with enemies on all sides and no other means of subsistence than penny-pinching international charity? The specter of a comparison with Lesotho, Swaziland or, worse still, with Gaza, already looms as a sinister, threatening reality. Piling error upon error, ever vacillating, ever appeasing, combining lack of a vision of the future with amnesia in relation to the past, the leaders of our *Common European Home* have cleared the way for the division in blood and fire of Bosnia-Herzegovina, the disintegration and extinction of a sovereign state, to be swallowed up like Abyssinia, Poland, Manchuria, or the Baltic states little over half a century ago. The perennial political-military logistics that date back to World War I, the moral and strategic blindness of the governments of Paris and London and their inability to foresee the danger of a general war in the Balkans will be judged by historians with the severity they deserve.

"We will not endorse any territorial gain by force of arms nor will we tolerate the continual and flagrant violation of international sanctions!" How often have we heard these empty words on the lips of Western leaders and negotiators, from the omnipotent Bush to the last clown in on the act? Promises swept away by the wind and not even a blush from those who formulated them! Milošević can feel proud of his achievements: in his cynical, cruel game of poker he has outwitted his opponents and always forced them to retreat. "We are now on the threshold of the final solution," he recently declared in Geneva. "All that remains to be sorted is simply a question of maps." In fact, the policy of non-intervention in Bosnia—the arms embargo on "the parties involved"—constitutes the most brutal example of intervention since the cabinets of London and Paris decisively contributed to the throttling and defeat of the Spanish Second Republic. In both cases, this hypocritical abstention—whoever witnesses a strangling such as that of Sarajevo and does nothing to stop it, is surely guilty of the crime of complicity—has worked against those who defended and defend democratic and legal institutions in favor of the aggressors and allies of Hitler and Mussolini or the standard-bearers of racial purification.

"To accept the partition is like allowing someone to enter your house, occupy more than half the rooms, steal your furniture, rape and murder your daughters, and ask you to sign on the dotted line," commented Bosnian vice president Ejup Ganic. Today the dismembering of his country along strictly ethnic lines is a reality. The three peoples who constituted Bosnia have been violently separated and the Geneva negotiators propose a confederation of three states "with free movement of people and goods." But who on earth would consider returning to a territory governed by people who burned their house down and tortured and executed their family? A demilitarized Muslim mini-state following Lord Owen's scheme would be at the mercy of its enemies. Six months after the Munich agreement—celebrated as a victory for peace by Chamberlain—Hitler entered Prague. Conscious of these new, atrocious "realities," the Bosnian presidency proposes putting its country under an international protectorate. But how can one even believe the validity of a surrender agreement if it too can change with time into another piece of wastepaper?

And what is to be done about Sarajevo? Ethnic cleansing would be impossible here, unless it were carried out building by building, floor by floor. The cosmopolitan nature of the city, fruit of the crucible of its four cultures, is a reality within the immediate family unit: there are tens of thousands of mixed marriages of Muslims, Croats, and Serbs. Must wife be separated from husband, dividing lines be established between stepbrothers, cousins, and sons-in-law? What should be the criteria in relation to children? What gene or blood should predominate? The father's or the mother's?

Two days before my departure I have dinner with Gervasio Sánchez and Alfonso Armada in the home of a friend of Gervasio's, a woman who lived some time ago in Madrid and has relatives in Spain. We park in a small yard where a group of men are chatting in the open apparently protected from enemy fire by an edifice overlooking the local river, but a few weeks ago a mortar flew over the building and demolished a house in this very spot! The neighbors on the stairs know Gervasio: they are mostly mixed families, still more closely knit by the horror of what is happening. One of them invited us to her home after our meal. The sun has sunk behind the mountains and an evening light illuminates the room where we settle down through a window space without glass or frame that looks directly out on the river and the besiegers' mountains. We sit in armchairs with half a dozen friendly, welcoming men and women who are deprived of the possibility of offering us, in keeping with their traditions of hospitality, even a simple glass of water. They have been like this for months, without light, gas, work, or hope, saving their strength for the daily transportation of water containers and the haphazard quest for a pretence of food. But they smile, and ask questions, as if life were following its normal pattern.

My attention immediately centers on a neat and tidy old lady who is all youthfulness, talk, and laughter despite her eighty-two years. She is delighted by our visit and enjoys the opportunity to chat with foreigners, like a Cinderella who has discovered her Prince Charming. She tells us about her Hungarian, Slovak, and Austrian origins, of her birth in a remote railway station in the middle of Bosnia. "That's why I've always dreamed about traveling," she says. "But my heart has never left Sarajevo." She now has a granddaughter in Poland and, although she cannot communicate with her because there is no postal service, she writes poetry to her. "Poetry?" "Yes," her family and neighbors chorus proudly and affectionately. "Would you like to read them to us?" The old lady has forgotten where she put them but she adds at once, she knows them by heart. "Couldn't you recite them to us?" She keeps us on tenterhooks for a moment with a delicious mixture of naïveté, guile, and coquettishness. It is now dark and someone lights the candle in its holder. The old lady's eyes are a pool of sweetness as she pours out the lines written for her granddaughter, which the interpreter translates as best she can: they tell her to live, to love, and take advantage of all that life grants her, but never to forget Sarajevo. "How long have you been writing for?" we ask her when she finishes. "Oh, for a long time" she smiles mischievously. "They are images and visions of the city." "Only of Sarajevo?" "I also wrote poems about Split. Water colors of Split." She recites these without waiting to be asked, in a gentle, nostalgic tone: they speak of the air, the sea, the sun, the twilight, the moon, the islands. "But I prefer the poems to Sarajevo." "Have you written anything about the war?" "No, I have never talked about politics, only of love and feeling I want my granddaughter to keep her memory of me and the city where she was brought up though she may never see us again."

We go downstairs by the glow of a cigarette lighter and, after bidding farewell to the assembly of shadows still gathered in the yard, we return to the hotel along Marshal Tito Avenue. The city is deserted, without pedestrians or traffic. One man is still pushing a cart loaded with containers, another runs across the road like a lunatic, fleeing imaginary shells or perhaps himself. Car headlights are dangerous because they offer snipers an easy target so you have to drive without them in the murky reaches of day.

Sarajevo is a cemetery by night, but the intermittent crackle of gunfire shatters the enclosed peace.

GOOD-BYE SARAJEVO

On the eve of my departure I breakfast with Susan Sontag before accompanying her to the small chamber theater where, by candlelight, she is going to start rehearsing her production of *Waiting for Godot.*

Just after my arrival in Sarajevo, seeing a besieged Sarajevo transformed into a concentration camp surrounded by invisible barbed wire—comparison with the Spanish civil war and the siege and bombing of Madrid struck me as unavoidable. Yes, there in the cover of the undergrowth, the buildings and nearby hills are "the cowards, the murderers, the fanatical adepts, the blind instruments of the darkest phantoms of history, the technicians of war, the skilled executioners of the human race" described by Antonio Machado. Yet how can one explain the abyss that lies between the leap in world consciousness in 1936 to defend a just cause despite its excesses and errors and the present apathy of intellectuals and artists, with the exception of a lucid minority, before the aggression, terror, and killing of the skilled disciples of Goebbels and Millán Astray? Where are the Hemingways, Dos Passos, Koestlers, Simone Weils, Audens, Spenders, Pazs, who didn't hesitate to take a stand and even fight, like Malraux and Orwell, by the side of a defenseless people under attack? Attempts by Susan Sontag and myself to bring writers of renown to Sarajevo have ended in fiasco. The ideological disarray created by the collapse of "real socialism," and the persistence of the strategies and reflex actions created by the cold war explain the phenomenon in part. We cannot plead ignorance: the journalists and photographers dispatched to Sarajevo and the war fronts have generally "covered" the news with exemplary honesty and courage. Despite that, public opinion vegetates in a kind of resigned stupor. Could this be the onset, we wonder, of exhaustion following on the proliferation of ethnic conflicts and insoluble wars in Asia, Africa, and the nations on the rim of the defunct

USSR? Or is it that the Bosnian presidency unsuccessfully begged help from the United States and the European Union, inducing many armchair intellectuals, used to clear distinctions between good and bad, to have its suspicions and admire Milošević's bold confronting of the arrogant, inept powers that today dominate the planet? Or can the gesticulating of the Security Council and resolutions of humanitarian aid have convinced the majority that our governments are doing all they can for that "hornets' nest in the Balkans"? or is it simply an uncontrollable aversion toward Islam? What can we make of intellectuals who forget the lessons of Auschwitz, and go, like Elie Wiesel, to the terrorized and starving ghetto to preach angelic "moderation on both sides"?

There are very few old-fashioned leftists and impenitent cosmopolitans able to understand, in the words of Michel Faher, editor of the New York magazine *Zone*, that "the defense of Sarajevo and the multicultural State springs not only from an elemental moral obligation and political reflex action," but also from a selfish need to "survive intellectually."

As in the Spanish civil war, the victorious camp has equally found its spokesmen: the picturesque British Hispanists, who confused Franco's victory dispatches with the deeds of the Cid Campeador, have aroused a much more sinister rival. The former Russian dissident Edward Limonov, supporter of national communism and close to the ideas of Le Pen, waxes ecstatically over "the extraordinary feeling of power conferred by a submachine gun," and takes up the words of the besiegers of Sarajevo in a foul-smelling report published in France: "This is the Third World War, the struggle between Christianity and Islam."

The Bosnian intellectuals who stay in Sarajevo against all the odds obsessively ask their companions: why so much cowardice and silence? Gathered around Senada Kreso, the Bosnian deputy minister for information, they evoke the happy, confident city of the films of Kusturica, the avant-garde theater, music, and cinema, an art and literature that were the beacon of Yugoslav intellectual life. Their universe suddenly collapsed in April 1992, two months after the "Yes" victory in the referendum on Bosnian independence boy-cotted by the Serbian ultranationalists.

"Whoever heard the first shells fired over Madrid by the rebel batteries, set up in the Casa de Campo, will always remember one of the most distasteful, distressing emotions . . . that can ever be experienced in life. There was the war, an obstinate, bestial onslaught, a war without the shadow of spirituality, its blind machines of destruction vomiting death coldly and systematically over an almost unarmed city, vilely stripped of all its fighting equipment," I had read these words days before in the volume of Machado that accompanied me on my journey, profoundly reliving the feelings of the poet canonized by our socialist politicians. As often happens in this world, they quote him but don't hear him!

A vague unease gradually fills the mind of the visitor as the day of departure approaches. What will become of the women and men whose company has been shared briefly but with an intensity not met before? What future awaits them, caught as they are in the mousetrap? On the occasion of a dinner in the hotel with one of those responsible for the humanitarian aid, well connected to the centers of political decision making in Washington and Brussels, I formulated two questions: "Can Sarajevo resist another winter?" The answer is emphatic: "No." "What will the UN and the European Union do if the ultras occupy the last bastions in the mountains, cut off the fragile supply of arms to the besieged, and submit the city to a final, savage bombard-ment?" "Apart from the odd newsworthy aerial punishment, absolutely nothing. Things will not change on the ground. Lord Owen will negotiate its division into two in Geneva and will give the lion's share to the Serbs."

How do you tell someone you love, after a series of med-ical tests, that it is cancer and that the doctors say there is no hope of living? Fleeing that feeling of overwhelming impo-tence, I devote the late hours of the afternoon to taking a quick look with Alma at the most beautiful areas of the city. It is a warm, sunny day, children are playing in the street and swimming in the river, the snipers are not shooting, and

Sarajevo seems to be bathed in an illusory peace. I try to hoard, avariciously, hastily, the most precious memories of my short but very long stay: the daily halts in the Morica Han, an old caravanserai in the Bascarsija, miraculously preserved from the bombing; tea in the little café next to the Sheher bridge, by the post with the warning PAZI SNAJPER, where a woman asked Alma if I was from Paris and wrote her daughter's telephone number with trembling fingers on my notepad: "Just tell her I'm still all right"; the inevitable wander round the Ottoman cemetery of Alifakovac, with its white stelas, turban-topped gravestones, and mausolea built like little temples with hexagonal roofs, gilt ball, and crescents; the almost magical appearance of a lady carrying water containers in both hands in the carriage entrance to the theater where Susan Sontag was about to start her rehearsals, wearing makeup and a cheerful floral dress, who spoke to me directly in French and praised Parisian politeness and good manners, though she only knew them by hearsay . . .

I review the elements in my daily apprenticeship. Anxiety and remorse at the sight of exhausted men and women who cannot possibly resist the winter without a major injection of humanitarian aid from the international community. Growing hatred of the bullet-proof vest—compulsory to board UN planes—which privileges me and separates me out from the rest of the besieged. Awareness of the futility of my suggestion to the poet Abdullah Sidran—how can I forget his energetic expression, trimmed beard, and patched, torn jeans? —about getting together a Bosnian literary anthology, provoked by his response: "An obituary is all you can write in Sarajevo today."

When the time comes, Alfonso and Gervasio fetch me from the hotel, we drive at top speed along Sniper Alley, pass through the labyrinth of UN controls, I sign the document that absolves the UN Protection Forces of all responsibility during the journey, I say good-bye already perched on the armored car. Then, the return trip to the airport with French soldiers, the maze of corridors till I reach the runway where the Hercules air shuttle is waiting. The porter at the Holiday

Inn entrusted me with a packet of letters to put stamps on and mail in Paris. Forewarned by my experience in the siege, I have hidden them in the folds of my plastic bag. Less cautious than myself, an American journalist who is leaving with me has an angry exchange with the supervising NCO who at the sight of post like mine, claims he has only the right to take out *five* letters. An extraordinary revelation: is the UN Security Force participating in the siege of Sarajevo?

Minutes afterwards, I'm out of the mousetrap: the plane takes off toward Split.

How can I sum up the feelings and emotions released by the city?

Life there acquires a vertiginous rhythm and intensity: hours are the equivalent of days; days, weeks; weeks, months. New friendships become deep and long-lived. Sincerity and a longing for truth take hold. One's sense of morality is refined and improved. Discarded concepts hurriedly cast on the dungheap of history are reborn with a new richness and strength: the need for commitment, the urgency of solidarity. Things that previously seemed important wane and lose substances; others slight in appearance suddenly acquire greatness and stand out as self-evident truths. Direct contact with the brutality and cowardice of the paladins of ethnic cleansing and the courage of the women and men who, defying sniper bullets and Serbian nationalist shelling, go out in search of water armed only with their faith and attachment to life, creates experiences and images that don't fade from the mind.

To live through these crucial hours is a terrible privilege. The journalists and members of the humanitarian organizations can attest to that: the tragedy of Bosnia is a unique way of knowing the luminous and the ignominious possibilities within the human race.

There they have rediscovered the vitality of values that gather dust or are ignored in our societies; sometimes in a very short space of time they have gained in rigor and authenticity.

Nobody can emerge unscathed from the descent into the hell of Sarajevo. The city's tragedy transforms the heart and perhaps the whole body of whoever witnesses it, into a bomb that is ready to explode in the moral security zones of those directly or indirectly responsible, wherever it can cause maximum damage.

ALGERIA

A BITTER AWAKENING

In the autumn of 1990 I traveled to Algeria to film a progam on the Saharan Ibadi for *Alquibla*, a series I wrote for Spanish television on aspects of Islam. In Ghardaia we stayed in a hotel inaugurated by President Chadli Bendjedid six months earlier: a gray, inhospitable, drab building already marked by symptoms of imminent decline. The rooms were small and uncomfortable, there were frequent cuts in the water supply, and the day the sound engineer left the tap turned on, he flooded half a hotel floor because of the lack of any adequate overflow outlet. When the cleaning superintendent was told of the accident, she scornfully shrugged her shoulders and said, "*Je m'en fous.*" None of her business! Neither was opening and closing the door the *business* of the porter who, rigged up like some gold-braided admiral, looked on impassively as an elderly French tourist struggled to push the door open with her shoulder, while wearily trailing her suitcase behind her; days later when the lock jammed and guests could neither go in nor out, the porter echoed the words of the cleaner: it was none of his business; if we wanted to complain we should go straight to the manager. I innocently surrendered a woollen jersey to the laundry service with comic consequences: after several futile attempts to recover it and after I'd overheard the Arabic exchanges of the receptionists ("Don't give it to him; tell him it's gone missing.") my garment was restored to me in miniature, exquisitely folded, as if tailor-made for one of Snow White's seven dwarves. The ostensibly off-duty track-suited employees wandering around the lobby discovered their real vocation the night one of them tiptoed stealthily after an Algerian theater director visiting our crew accompanied by three Canadian actors, that is, until the moment he began to enter one of the actresses' bedrooms, whereupon he was summoned to reception and threatened with a night in the police station. But the culmination of these instances of demoralization and bloody-mindedness was the famous telephone. Of the half-dozen phone booths standing in the lobby, apparently only one worked: a queue of motley individuals waited their turn in front of it while the others remained forlornly empty. I soon became impatient at the endless waiting and decided with no high hopes to try my luck in another booth: I picked up the receiver, waited for the tone, dialed my number, and got straight through to Paris. Now the cat was out of the bag: the telephone being so assiduously and faithfully courted was like the "saint" evoked by the protagonists of the *Journey to Turkey* who "let you have a free ride." You only had to slip in a dinar to enjoy unlimited communication with Algiers, Paris, Madrid, Riad, or Cairo and even have the dinar, so fruitfully loaned out, returned at the end of the call. During our weeklong shoot I spotted in the line of people "in the know," servants of a Kuwaiti or Saudi prince who had come to practise the art of falconry, tourists and guests from a number of countries, hotel employees and security guards, even the odd policeman. And it was all happening opposite reception, under the hotel manager's nose! In a country rent by so much internal discord, people could at least agree on one thing: the need to trick and defraud the state.

How had things come to such a sorry pass? I called up tumultuous images from my first journey to Algeria in July 1962: the ecstatic celebrations after the hard-earned victory in the struggle for independence, the atmosphere of fraternity where European supporters of the revolution were welcome, the almost general expectation of a more just, more democratic, freer future. With Jean Daniel, Gisèle Halimi, and other friends and champions of the Algerian cause, we walked through the working-class areas of Babel-Oued and the Casbah, attended a meeting addressed by President Ben Bella in a football field, traveled to Blida and Tipaza, visited a farm abandoned by *pieds noirs* and expropriated under the agrarian reform, shook hands with the voluble, charismatic president while Boumedien, in the background, looked on, as I remember him, enigmatic and silent like a bird stalking its prey. To tell the truth, the political situation already displayed ominous signs of a return to the precolonial past, to the patrimonial system of the Ottoman beys; clan warfare, ethnic and regional rivalries, the open or latent opposition of some *wilayat*, nepotism, the entry of the military into the political arena. Ait Ahmed, whom we visited in his fief in the Kabylia, was at odds with the government. Ben Khedda, the former president of the Provisional Government of the Republic of Algeria (GPRA) had resigned from his post after Ben Bella's arrival on the shoulders of the army. Boudiaf, who silently criticised the direction events were taking, was about to experience imprisonment at the hands of his peers after five years in French jails.

On subsequent trips to Algeria after Boumedien's military coup I was able to witness at firsthand the withering of the political project, the neglect of agriculture, bureaucratic despotism, an all-powerful police force, a strategy of forced industrialization doomed to failure, and a Bismarkian obsession with converting the country into the dominant power in North Africa through its prestige abroad and leadership role in the Non-Aligned Countries movement. My contacts with North African workers who had emigrated to France enabled me to hear the first, really serious alarm bells: from the mid-sixties, while Moroccan and Tunisian workers sent their savings back to Morocco and Tunisia to build a home or open a shop, Algerians kept their money in France and preferred to bring their family there. That lack of confidence in the future anticipated the next phase: In Algeria, they said, individual initiative leads nowhere, the bureaucrats are incompetent, the Front de Libération Nationale (FLN) is creating a generation of youths who have forgotten what work is and are conditioned to rely on welfare handouts. The gap widened between the official and real value of the dinar year by year: although the official rate was slightly above the franc, my acquaintances suggested they could get double or triple the sum they would get in France. The year Boumedien died, on a trip to Beni Drar, in the Beni Snassen area near the Moroccan frontier, my Moroccan hosts showed me bundles of 100 dinar notes that Algerian smugglers gave them on behalf of traders or bureaucrats in Maghnia or Tlemsen to be changed in Oujda at a third of their value: 33 dirhams. I had no need to have recourse to political analysis or unreliable statistics: experience showed me the harsh realities hidden by "revolutionary" myths and demagogy.

I often wondered how so many left-wing essayists and politicians could have fallen into the trap of considering the regime of Boumedien and even of Chadli Bendjedid as the epitome of progressive, democratic politics. Did they consider its clearly visible ravages to be momentary failings with respect to its "essential" worth? When in 1976 I had recently recovered my right to an opinion and dared express the view that the Moroccan regime, with all its defects, appeared preferable to the one in Algeria inasmuch as it was open to correction, whereas the FLN was devastating its country, the salvo of insults and righteous responses that greeted my articles was as strident as it was unanimous. It was the period when the present leaders of the Spanish government—then in opposition—returned from their *journeys by hot-air balloon* to Algeria like Alice from Wonderland, proclaiming that they shared the same ideals as the FLN, praising to the skies "the revolutionary gains" of a society on the edge of the abyss. How could they not notice the approaching cataclysm? Was their reading of reality so blinkered by ideology that they mistook windmills for castles?

When the events of October 1988 and the bloody repression that was unleashed finally opened the eyes of the regime's friends and supporters, they discovered to their dismay the magnitude of the disaster, as did an Algerian press finally liberated from its chains.

When Algeria won independence, it was a large exporter of agricultural food products, it had the best infrastructure on the continent after South Africa, and the sale of hydrocarbons comprised only 12 percent of its exports. The policy of enforced industrialization and the sustained neglect of agriculture transformed the country into a single-exporting state within five years. In 1988, 95 percent of its income came from hydrocarbons; 80 percent of food consumed had to be imported. Boumedien and his advisers believed that the sale of oil and natural gas would allow them to carry through their giant projects and would subsidize feeding the population. That was possible after the Israeli-Egyptian war and the sudden increase in the price of crude oil. But the gradual fall in oil prices over the following decade drastically reduced the inflow and the foreign capital markets that had been so generously open to Algeria suddenly shut their gates. Meanwhile the population had increased from 11 million to 25 million inhabitants; large public enterprises functioned at a 30 percent capacity; in spite of a large number of subsidies to those who were technically unemployed, the unemployment figure reached 20 percent—mostly young people—and is today 25 percent of the active population. At the end of the eighties, everything seemed to combine to paralyse the country after twenty years of debt accumulation and overspending ($100,000 million buried in enormous industrial cemeteries): interest payments on the debt of $26,000 million absorbs 80 percent of the profits from the sale of hydrocarbons; foreign investors stay clear of an unstable country fettered by a bungling, corrupt bureaucracy; shortages and the spiraling prices of ordinary consumer goods, urban overcrowding caused by population growth and rural exodus following on from the destruction of the agricultural system—on average, seven people per dwelling and three per room—inflame the impatient tempers of a people exasperated by a lack of basic commodities, by water and electricity cuts, and the collapse of the transport system. In recent years income per capita has fallen from $2,700 to $1,400. Moroccan agriculture caters for 70 percent of national consumption, but Algerian farms can only meet 2 percent of demand. "The old bread basket of the Romans in the times of Livy has been sacrificed," wrote Zakya Daud in *Le Monde Diplomatique*. "Where the ancient civilisation of the olive reigned supreme, people now cook with imported rape or sunflower seed oil." The mass of young unemployed—the *hittists* or street loafers—with no schooling or future were, in 1988, a powder keg ready to explode. The devastating effects of a quarter of a century of corruption, waste, and a single party system were clear to see: a cultural and moral desert, aimlessness, a loss of any sense of identity, violent flows of unchannelled energies, hatred of the *nomenklatura*. Months after the crushing of the demonstrations on the streets of Algiers and Oran, thousands of young people were shouting in football stadiums: *"rana daya'in, idduna Filistin!* We're lost, send us to Palestine!" Soon they would begin the war or *jihad* of their dreams in their own country. Their marginalization and implacable hatred for the system led them fatally to the bellicose, avenging ranks of the Islamic Salvation Front (Front Islamic du Salut, FIS).

ISLAM AND POLITICS

The first ethnographic studies of Algerian Islam during the reign of Napoleon III—the work of French military men and administrators like Louis Rinn, Depont, and Coppolani—offer valuable insights into the workings of Arab-Berber society after the fall of the Ottoman Beys, despite the fact that they were explicitly instructed to separate and classify different tendencies and affinities according to their degree of deference or defiance in regard to the colonizing power. The Sufi brotherhoods, pilgrimages to the tombs of saints, the power of the marabouts, division of the country into *makhzen* and independent tribes, and the influence of the religious nobility (the *shurfa*), and so forth, are quite similar to those in neighboring Morocco; the reality of a popular, pragmatic, superstitious Islam against which the purifying efforts of the *salafiya* in Morocco struggled in vain. The French used every means to suppress this spontaneity and "fanaticism"—a portmanteau word designating oppressed nationalist sentiment and the existence of "anarchic" brotherhoods and *zawiyas* opposed to modernization—in favor of an official, regulated, submissive Islam. Although the insurrections led by some sheiks in 1871 and 1881 were mercilessly crushed, the colonial administration bought the loyalty of numerous families of marabouts and members of the *shurfa*, transforming their members into qadis, imams, and intermediaries in their service. Their modernizing project implied the harnessing of Islam to the tutelage of a Jacobin lay state, the gradual de-arabization of culture and uprooting of representative popular myths and symbols. But this process of Westernization had its limits: the ones set by colonialism. The modernizers were not seeking to enact equality between colonizers and colonized. The Algerian assimilationist movement, under the leadership, after World War I, of a grandson of the Emir Abdelkadir, met with the outright opposition of the French. The republican slogan—freedom, equality, fraternity—made sense in the metropolis but not in its North African *départements*. The contradictions and iniquities of the French colonial presence had lasting consequences: they cut off the mass of the Algerian people from their traditional roots yet did not integrate them into a state with equal shares of rights and responsibilities. The Frenchified elites and urban bourgeoisie fought for more than two decades for legal equality, then for autonomy, and finally for interdependence within the framework of the French Republic: that was more or less the way the politics of individuals like Ferhat Abbas evolved. Persistent rejections from Paris, dictated by the suicidal blindness of the *pieds-noirs*, opened the road to independence movements, first with Messali Hadj and then the FLN.

The onslaught against Algerian cultural and religious practices went on for more than a century. In the thirties Emile Dermengheim could still describe in very striking terms the worship of saints and Sufi ceremonies in different parts of the country, reminding me of what one can experience nowadays in Morocco. Thousands of the faithful were still drawn to the vast expanse of the beautiful sanctuary in Tlemcen, a masterpiece of Almohad art, where Sidi Boumedien—the great Andalusian mystic, essential link with the *silsila* or chain of initiation of the majority of North African brotherhoods, patron of the city as well as author of popular *qasidas* and *zajals* whose repertory later included the *melhun* lies buried; impressive processions of brotherhoods playing musical instruments and dancing ecstatically gathered at the end of Ramadan in the neighboring village that goes by his name, to celebrate Id al Kabir and commemorate the birth of the Prophet. The attempt to create a Frenchified elite as a simple transmission belt for their colonial power went together with the separating out and exclusive promotion of a functional, state-subsidized Islam. Scorned by the modernists with their new lay values, popular piety flourished as the expression of an identity which, though repressed, remained vigorous and intense. This destructive enterprise was completed in the name of socialism and progress by those who took power in

Algeria after the resignation of Ben Khedda in September 1962: the pilgrimages to Sidi Abderrahman Tha'alabi, the patron saint of Algiers, to Sidi M'hamed in Belcourt, to Sidi M'bar in Buzarka were subject to bureaucratic harassment or simply banned. Like France, the Popular Democratic Republic of Algeria also wanted a formal, official Islam, freed of any of the "obscurantist" religious manifestations from a backward countryside where people would soon be shaken up by a disastrous agrarian revolution and forced to emigrate and crowd into the suburbs of the big cities. In 1991, during a film shoot in Oran, my friends from the arts faculty told me that gatherings and acts of worship in front of the tomb of their patron saint were only authorized in 1989, in the wake of the recent October insurrection. Since then, the burning by FIS members of several mausolea and hermitages—Sidi Kada in Mascara, Sidi M'hamed Benauda in Rezilan and so on—as well as damage inflicted on those in Algiers and other cities—shows that the acculturation project is unfortunately carrying out its task under another guise. Often, when reading about events in a self-destructing Algeria torn by huge problems of identity and a series of supposedly enlightened despotic governments, I have recalled Dermengheim's lucid and prophetic warnings: "Renewal and progress within Islam will not happen through the adoption of merely formal aspects or by copying outside developments but only by revitalising its most profound values. The opponents of the worship of saints are no doubt engaged in a worthy attempt to liberate, educate and purify; but by moving away from the sources of spiritual life one runs the risk of not only purifying but of damaging the substrata of collective emotions. Constrained in that way, they will tend to erupt in blind fury." This was written more than half a century ago: events of today starkly reveal how apposite his words still are.

Contrary to what people generally think, it is not Islam that has incorporated the ideologies of the Western world and the values they project: these ideologies have used Islam to prove the validity of their liberal, democratic or socialist principles. In the Arab world, modernizing, lay doctrines did not spring up from within their own societies as they did in Europe: they were introduced from the outside, in the shadow of an imperial power which applied them in the metropolis but refused to grant them to their colonized or "protected" peoples. In order to impose them successfully, the modernizing leaders of independence had recourse to *hadith* and quotations taken from Koranic *surahs*. Nasser and Boumedien are the best examples of this kind of manipulation. In this way, the nationalist and "socialist" leaders of the sixties and the seventies had at least one point of contact with their traditionalist and conservative rivals: they invoked religion in order to keep in touch with the masses.

One must always bear in mind that there is not a single Islam. Muslim governments can be totalitarian or liberal, adepts of the ideas of social progress or locked into rigid, anachronistic traditions. The Koran justifies the legitimacy of traditional monarchies, whether the open variety (Morocco, Jordan), or fundamentalist (Saudi Arabia), but it also encompasses their bitterest enemies (Algeria, Egypt). Some underline community and social aspects; others stress respect for the Sunna and quietist values. In general, "conservatives" opt for technical, material, and scientific progress but never abandon the return to cultural and religious sources of identity, "cleansed" of all contamination by the West. They often cite Japan as an example of the resolution of this apparent dichotomy.

The Association of Algerian Ulema, created in 1931 by Sheih Ben Badis, began a reformist movement whose influence persisted to the beginning of the insurrection: this movement, on a par with the zealous *salafiya* in Morocco, later came under the influence of populist tendencies inspired by the doctrines of Hasan el Banna, founder of the movement of the Muslim Brotherhood. From the beginning, the struggle for independence forced its leaders to use Islam as a recruiting banner: the war against France was thus both a patriotic and Muslim national enterprise against the oppression of the *nasrani* (the religious designation of Europeans). Although the FLN Federation in France, supported by Boudiaf, proposed the creation of a lay state, such a suggestion was ignored for the same reasons that, decades earlier, the Paris government refused to apply to Muslims the 1904 law concerning the separation of religion and the state, sought by *ulema* who wanted to create an autonomous religious space. When the FLN leaders in 1962 proclaimed Islam as the "religion of the state," they wanted to ensure control of the management and direction of religious affairs: imams were to be civil servants. Mosques and religious foundations had to collaborate with the regime's literacy campaigns and to accept that Third World progressive politics were at one with the revelations of the Book.

Those who believed wholeheartedly in Boumedien's socialism didn't understand that it was a capitalist response to an absence or almost total absence of capitalism: the creation of a state capitalism whose burden was to industrialize and modernize Algerian society. From the very first the financial-political oligarchy that grew under the wings of the single party reflected the crudest materialism in its way of life. Alien to all the religious and cultural traditions swept aside by French colonialism and three decades of FLN dictatorship and corruption, it does not devote part of its fortune, like the *shurfa* or nobility of yesteryear, to religious foundations, libraries, or Islamic schools: it pours it into the acquisition of villas, cars, trips to France, and a sickening display of high-society living and regular attendance at casinos and nightclubs. The contrast between their lifestyle and that of the marginalized masses squashed into the poor areas of the cities and shantytowns on the outskirts becomes intolerable for the latter. "Socialism," they begin to say out loud, is a ruse invented by the *nomen klatura* to take over the positions of authority once occupied by the colonizers. The "French Party"—whose language this privileged layer prefers to use—are thus put on a level with the *pieds noirs* and their *harkis*. For young people born after independence, this struggle has opened up a new chapter: from now on it is a fight between Algerians.

From the end of the seventies, the affirmation of Islam in political terms conceals and blocks out its spiritual, cultural and historical values. Reference to the *shari'a* and to the sunna—or to the holy imams within Iranian Shi'ism—becomes an essential element in legitimizing government projects. In other words, Islam conceived as a faith, as a deep personal experience or ethic, is replaced by a simplifying doctrine that ignores individual efforts to interpret the text of the Koran, and restricts itself to the condemnation of the regimes in power as "unholy." For a time, nationalism combined nostalgia for the past and revolutionary hopes for a more just world. After the latter vanished with the eclipse and failure of "socialist" military leaders (Nasser, Boumedien), the sectors marginalized by a Western-style modernity cling to the former in their attempts to leave behind the social and cultural wasteland where they rotted. The human swathes of the faithful prostrated outside the mosques of Cairo or Algeria that so disturb Westerners is less an expression of fervor than an act of protest. The rejection or ignoring of the greatness of Arab culture in both its mystic and rationalist dimensions—so manifest in Saudi *wahhabism* and Algerian Islamism—is compensated for by the reduction of religion to a set of external practices and a strict application of Koranic teachings (banning the consumption of alcohol, rules on dress and so on). Whenever I have mentioned this impoverishment—privileging the social and political over the contemplative, theological, and poetic dimension—to any FIS supporter or member, the reply has always been evasive: "Our people demand bread and justice, not the books of Ibn Khaldun or Ibn Arabi."

The subordination of official Islam to the regime ended with the death of Boumedien. A new generation of imams, influenced by radical Islamist tendencies, centered its proselytizing in the neglected areas springing up around the big cities, created hundreds of mosques or spaces to pray with or without state authorization, made its new rallying cry the struggle against corruption and "decadent customs" and the total Arabization of the country. Until then the government had played a skillful balancing act between the Marxists who would later make up the Socialist Vanguard Party (PAGS) and the Islamists, yielding to the latter when circumstances advised (for example, in the elaboration of a highly conservative Family Code). This balancing act was ended by the entry onto the political stage of the excluded masses organized by the FIS. In 1982 the Front broke definitively with the FLN: Sultani, Sahnun, and Abbasi Madani went to jail for the first time. Madani, hitherto quite unknown, was soon to win renown.

THE CAUSES OF THE ISLAMIC
SALVATION FRONT

When Boumedien died, the mosques became the only arenas for open opposition to the regime. In the working-class districts of the Casbah, Babel-Oued, and El Harrash, where families of five or six sometimes are jammed together in a single room, young people, unqualified or possessing worthless certificates, pace the streets with no hope of work or of emigration to Europe, no diversions or adequate sports facilities. The 100,000 new dwellings promised every year by the new president dwindle to 20,000, while housing needed to give decent shelter to the homeless are calculated at around the 3 million mark. The people living in shantytowns have no schools, clinics, or welfare offices for the unemployed. As far as they are concerned the state doesn't exist: the youth have been abandoned to their fate.

The Islamists have cleverly filled the power vacuum. Subsidized by Saudi Arabia until their hesitant support for Saddam Hussein forced on them by the rank and file, Madani, Belhaj, and the movement's leaders are gradually weaving an alternative system of social support, organizing and mobilizing the marginalized with their promises of radical change, slowly re-Islamizing society, cleaning out the drug and alcohol traffickers from decaying ghettos and districts, and imposing their own educational model within miserably impersonal, acculturated spaces. Authorized or not, mosques are shooting up like mushrooms: alongside private and state *aljamas*—where sermons are controlled by Front de Libération Nationale (FLN) religious affairs leaders—"popular" and "free" oratories are emerging. As Ahmed Rouadjia writes in his work *Les frères et la mosquée*, "There exist thousands of hidden mosques, exactly like the parallel market for goods, escaping all control inasmuch as they operate in the shelter of basements, garages and shanty towns on the edge of the big conurbations." Simultaneously, shortages and breakdowns in the state education system have led to the siphoning of children and adolescents into improvized Koranic schools unsupervised by officialdom. On university campuses, Islamists evict from their offices or meetings "Marxist," "atheist" students or those belonging to the "French Party." Mixed gatherings or parties are banned, girls are pressured into covering their hair, and the white *kamis* and emblematic beards win new adepts by the day. In such a traditionally liberal city as Oran, in autumn 1990 the municipal authorities, on the advice of the FIS, banned the holding of public *rai* concerts: women could go to the cinema only on the day reserved "for families" and before dusk had totally disappeared from the streets. The contrast with Tunisia or Morocco could not be more stark.

The *jihad*, or call for a holy war against "corrupt leaders" and "Frenchified intellectuals" is the Islamists' most efficient mobilizing weapon because it appeals to a deeply rooted collective imagery. The millions of unemployed, excluded from the system and offended by the oligarchy's luxurious lifestyle, find their only succor in messianic hopes. Thus, Islamism becomes a common denominator with which all the marginalized can identify. The FIS can invoke not only the example of Iran but also that of several Sunni preachers from the golden age of Islam who, like Zayd Ibn Ali or Al Yazid, denounced the depravation and arrogance of the Ummayad and Abbasid Caliphates. Like Communists in past decades, it garners the fruits of social frustration and feelings of injustice that have accumulated after the failure of socialist models and the later "ruthless opening up." But the present violence — the weapon of terrorism which, and this is something new within Islam and contrary to its teachings, doesn't even forgive defenseless women — is not the result of extremist religious discourse, but, like Irish Catholicism, rises from a state of political and cultural oppression. In reality, the FIS preaches a highly conservative social program — the imams' defense of private property against the Agrarian Revolution of the seventies earned them considerable support among traders and rural property owners, which they dress up in a religious language that is easily accessible to the large mass of dispossessed. In the present circumstances of social breakdown, a significant section of the Algerian people judge corruption and nepotism to be worse evils than blind terrorist violence.

Shari'a as a system of government is the FIS's proclaimed goal in its struggle to win power. But is an Islamic state from the times of the Prophet an example of millennial utopianism, as its enemies maintain, or is it a real solution to the problems and ills of society? In fact, how can one establish a definite link between the Koranic text and the corpus of the *hadith*, of the *Sunna*, and purely political decision making? The Koran doesn't specify any particular form of government. Then why should what is described in Europe and by Algerian intellectuals as "fundamentalist," "reactionary," "totalitarian," or "theocratic" prevail over the rest?

The FIS victory in the municipal elections on 12 June 1990—the first election held in Algeria in the framework of the multiparty state inscribed in the new 1989 constitution—shook to the very core the foundations of the government of Chadli Bendjedid and its leader Mouloud Hamrouche. Taking advantage of the divisions and the democratic opposition boycott (Ait Ahmed's Front of Socialist Forces—FFS) and the general discrediting of the FLN, the FIS swept to power in more than half of the town halls—thus winning control of the Popular Communal Assemblies (APC)—was victorious in most reasonably sized cities and got solid backing in the capital cities of Algiers, Oran, and Constantine. As the most clearsighted observers note, this massive vote (59 percent) is more of a *vote to punish the FLN than a positive vote for the model of society invoked by the FIS*. If the savage criticisms and avenging Islamist discourse in respect to the corruption, embezzling of public funds, favoritism, oppression, and arrogance of the single party and its military backers are on target, its ideas for improvement and change are quite vague and unreal. With no experience in the management of public affairs, their promises of housing and jobs for everyone, school buildings, and economic modernization do not take into account the hard facts of reality: the bankruptcy and dependency of the Algerian state. Between 12 June 1990 and 23 May 1991—the date of Abbasi Madani's call for a general strike against government maneuvering in the runup to the legislative elections of 27 June and in favor of early presidential elections—the changes wrought locally by the ACP were quite modest: bars were closed, musical shows stopped, sometimes violent campaigns took place for "feminine decency" and against the ubiquitous satellite disks that "enable one to tune into Western pornography." From the founding of the FIS to the events of June 1991, neither Madani nor his *majlis al-shura* (consultative assembly) elaborated a real social political program, nor did they call a congress to discuss any such thing. Questioned about that by the press, all Madani would say was that it would meet after he had formed a government. . . . The FIS's opposition to "rigged" legislative elections led to real insurrection recalling the one in October 1988: Molotov cocktails, tear gas, and barricades. Ali Belhaj, the charismatic imam from the mosque in Bab el-Oued propeled tens of thousands into the streets to demonstrate by shouting: "Down with the Charter and the Constitution! Long live the Word of God! Long live the Word of the Prophet!" Although the government seemed impotent and paralysed, the FIS strutted victoriously through the center of the capital. Despairing youths, victims of the defunct social project of the FLN, their only spiritual sustenance *rejla* manliness combined with neighborhood spirit, suddenly ceased to be petty criminals on the make and were transformed, thanks to the sermons of the Islamists, into fighters for the new *jihad*. The *hogra* (contempt) they suffer and the endless arrogance of those in power can be explained easily: all the misery and iniquities are the result of neglect of the teachings of the Koran, forgetting of its rules about the just distribution of riches, about social behavior and values. The constitution is one more ploy to disguise the forces of oppression. Islam is based on the *shura* (consultation) and strict application of the *shari'a*. On 3 June the forces of law and order violently dispersed demonstrators, arrested Madani, Belhaj, and others in the FIS leadership, and began huge roundups of Islamists and searches in the poor districts where they have their support.

Alternating the stick and the carrot, the government of Sid Ahmed Ghozali promised to keep to the legislative election calendar fixed first in October and then in December. Retrospectively, the military and their democratic allies, opposed to any agreement with the Islamists, criticized this concession as a new link in a chain of errors leading to the cycle of violence into which Algeria was plunging. Wouldn't it have been easier to break off the electoral process in June on the pretext of the FIS insurrection rather than to allow it to appear as a "martyr" to democracy and the subsequent verdict from the ballot box, with the Islamic leaders in jail, subject to trial and severe prison sentences? Chadli Bendjedid's regime had no one to talk to. Like a fabled beast from the *Arabian Nights,* once the head was severed, the body didn't die, but took on a new life. Islamism already impregnated every sector of society, organized its clandestine militia, acted like a state within a state. In autumn 1991, the first armed groups, apparently trained by Afghanistan veterans and survivers of the extremist guerrilla force *Takfir wa Hijra,* embarked on a campaign of assaults on barracks and army harrassment. The military high command viewed with growing unease the worsening situation and Chadli's vacillations. The internal divisions in the country were often reflected within families: families with more than one son in the FIS and others in the police or the army were not uncommon. The specter of civil war and fratricide in the strict sense of the word was hovering over society and would soon swoop to take its prey.

The first round of legislative elections in December confirmed the hopes of some and the fears of others: the FIS won a majority. The predictable result of the second round guaranteed it the comfortable two-thirds majority in the future National Assembly necessary to modify the 1989 constitution and legally establish another according to the *shari'a.* That victory galvanized the anxieties of the armed forces and a *nomenklatura* fearful for its future and the loss of its privileges. These apprehensions were shared by a number of the political parties, trade unions, lay intellectuals, and women's associations. The example of what happened in Iran was on everyone's mind. On 12 January 1992, after days of tense waiting and backroom dealing, President Chadli Bendjedid appeared ashen-faced before the television cameras to announce his resignation. On the following day, the government suspended the electoral process. The experiment in democracy had failed.

Jettisoning their self-righteous lectures on law and ethics and their criticism of "the inability of Arabs to organise free elections" Western governments and news media almost unanimously supported the coup d'état. The specter of the Islamic threat brandished by the press for some years—in bellicose headlines about the "black tide of Islam" or "Allah's Hordes"—led them to approve unreservedly the liquidation of democracy on the pretext that it was in serious danger. Minorities, whether lay, Marxist, or the Berber radicals in the Grouping for Culture and Democracy led by Said Saadi also applauded: no freedom for the enemies of freedom. But these reactions stemmed from analyses dictated by emotion and fear and not from any knowledge of the Islamist phenomenon or of whatever causes were nurturing it.

Obviously, the coming to power of the FIS would have represented a serious threat to freedoms that had been won in difficult circumstances in October 1988, but the conditions in which it came to power would have sorely limited its ability to apply its program. Algeria's debt, its financial dependency on Japanese and European creditors, economic chaos, and the hostility of the army would have constituted almost insurmountable obstacles. What is more; the lack of experience in government and social measures on behalf of the rank and file would have precipitated the crisis and brought on catastrophe. Its inability to meet its electoral promises was entirely predictable. Within less than a year of government tightly controlled by its enemies, the FIS would have lost a good deal of its credibility.

Recourse to the sword was, then, a cure worse than the sickness. For thirty years, FLN "socialism" had discredited the ideas of the left in the eyes of the people. The annulment of the elections greeted gleefully by "Democrats" showed in turn the emptiness and elitism of the option they were defending. As in other historical circumstances, the latter showed their natural aversion to respecting the people's will that was alien to their ideas and way of life and whose avenging demands questioned their status and enlightening role. We cannot help but draw the parallel between their attitude and that of "enlightened" Peninsular intellectuals who welcomed Joseph Bonaparte's reforms and constitution, which developed without real popular support—because the masses lacked a political culture—with respect to the people's religious and patriotic reactions, hostile to foreign ideas and in favor of absolutism and the power of the Church.

Deprived of their only source of legitimacy—the ballot box—the military, their allies in an FLN in disarray, and the small lay parties filled the power vacuum by finding a makeweight in *historical legitimacy*. The newly created High Council of State (HCS) offered its helm to a symbol brought back from the dead: the old independence leader Mohamed Boudiaf.

FROM BOUDIAF'S MARTYDOM TO THE
SECOND BATTLE OF ALGIERS

By halting the electoral process, the powers-that-be broke off
channels of communication with their real interlocutors and
fanned the flames of violence that increases daily. The
attempt at dialogue and unity without taking into account the
popular will then favorable to Islamists led the country into a
kind of political autism that divides it in half: on the one
hand, the reality of a majority party with no legal right to
existence; on the other, the fiction of a legal structure lacking
any credible base. The call to Boudiaf was the only way to
preserve the legitimacy of the revolution's historic legacy, a
final attempt to drape an immaculate cloak of honesty over
three decades of negligence, corruption, and nepotism.

Despite his ennobling presence and the expectations his
return raised among the sectors of the population that were
tired of the FLN and intimidated by the FIS, the Council of
State that Boudiaf presided over was born tainted by its original sin. As Abdennur Ali Yahya, a lawyer in the High Court
of Algiers and a well-known defender of human rights, later
wrote in *Le Monde,* "What right has a minority from the old
regime, bolstered by another tiny minority of 'democrats,'
removed by universal suffrage, to rule over the country and
force itself upon the vast majority of Algerians? . . . Democracy
is not the expression of a minority—that smacks strangely of
European rule over Algeria—propelled into the limelight of
power by the media it manipulates and attempting to occupy
the political arena despite being massively rejected at the ballot box." After twenty-five years of exile in Morocco did
Boudiaf foresee the destiny that awaited him when he was
called upon to preside over the Council of State? His political
record—years of clandestine struggle, French prisons, a brief
period in the Algerian Popular Republican Government
(GRPA) led by Ben Khedda, resignation in August 1962,

imprisonment ten months later, and so on—created an image of integrity, of a man of principles comparable in a way to the image of a Mendès-France in France. A glance at his declarations and warnings to the political class from the proclamation of independence to his arrest by Ben Bella bear witness to striking lucidity and prophetic gifts: "Those who talk endlessly about agrarian reform, industrialisation, a single party and other wonderful projects are but ignorant demagogues. . . . To talk of socialism means opposing any hint of despotism, all militarism, all subversion or underhand activity that will sow confusion, demobilize the masses, and prepare the advent of a dictatorial regime." During his exile, he had carefully followed the evolution of the single party and vigorously denounced its shortcomings, and had shown his clearsightedness when with the former presidents of the GRPA he condemned Boumedien's hegemonist policies in relation to decolonizing the Sahara. I had the opportunity to meet him in the seventies in Rabat and admired the subtlety of his analyses and remarkable intellectual curiosity: in prison he had learned Spanish and spoke knowledgeably about various classical and contemporary Spanish novels.

Boudiaf came to rescue Algeria from the abyss into which it had fallen; but the people who brought him on their shoulders only did so to save the system that was directly responsible for the catastrophe. Civil war had begun: the two sides were locked—are locked—in a relentless confrontation and he belonged to neither. Unknown to the generations born or brought up after independence, in the eyes of many he seemed to be a phantom, an apparition from another era. Very few doubted his goodwill and honesty: his exemplary life provided ample evidence of those qualities. But did he really know what a merciless lions' den he was entering? One day a dispassionate history of his short-lived presidency will tell us the truth. His first steps in office reveal the caution and hesitancy of someone testing the ground, testing for quicksands that may be about to swallow him up. Recourse to a series of advisers of *beur* origin from France showed his radical distrust of the Algerian political class and a desire to streamline the administration and democratize the state. However, his attempts to struggle against Islamist extremism and the political/financial mafia were doomed to failure from the outset. Although Boudiaf embodied the *legality* of power—a doubtful legality, remember, because of its flawed source—the *reality* of power continued to be the army. His margin for maneuver was clearly limited and when some of his sponsors glimpsed a direct threat to their privileges in his attempts to restore morality to public life they probably decided to get rid of him. Who was behind his executioner, a member of his personal bodyguard and a supposed Islamist? The official version of events was immediately belied by public opinion: the assassination bore the mark of a government faction and its awesome "parallel services."

In a moving article, "The Day President Boudiaf Died" (*Mediterraneans*, summer 1993), journalist Akram Belkaid eloquently pointed the finger at those who had masterminded the attack: "Who will one day have the courage to accuse those really responsible, those who after independence confiscated the freedom we had regained and forced upon us a spurious system of education, the degrading mental habits of a 'nation of beggars'?" Boudiaf's *martyrdom* is in any case one of the most painful pages in the recent history of Algeria: the symbolic gesture by Hasiba Bulmerka—the sprinter who won a gold medal in the Olympic Games in Barcelona—of dedicating her victory to him constituted posthumous recognition of his figure by a younger generation that never knew him but recognized the significance of his sacrifice.

The murder of the president of the Council of State and his replacement by Ali Kafi did not modify the key factors in the political equation. To tell the truth, it made them worse: the appointment of Belid Abdeslam, the visible head of the political-financial oligarchy of the FLN, to lead the government and of General Khaled Nezzar, a supporter of outright war against the Islamists, to the Ministry of Defense, took place in a climate of severe social and political crisis. The necessary restoration of morality to public life and sorting out an economy that had been bled dry—the priorities of Mohamed

Boudiaf—we postponed in favor of the struggle against terrorism. By sentencing Abbasi Madani and Ali Belhaj to twelve years' imprisonment the government has not only deprived itself of the possibility of talking to them: it increases the radicalization of the Islamic Salvation Front (FIS) and the disturbing fragmentation of its rank and file. The massive arrests of thousands of members and supporters of the Islamist movement, sometimes of ordinary demonstrators, and their internment in detention centers in the Sahara, has triggered urban terrorism and rural guerrilla warfare. Armed actions— begun in the autumn of 1991—are spreading at a dizzying rate: sabotage, attacks, ambushes, arson, and the "execution' of soldiers and police. The Armed Islamic Movement (MIA), the successor to its Afghan homonym created by the legendary Bouyali brothers in the era of Chadli Bendjedid, has reappeared under the leadership of his lieutenants, Chebuti and Meliani. In spite of the differences that exist between the *Salafi* leaders in prison or exile and the new *Algerianist* leadership, the organizers of the 1991 December electoral campaign have come together in their support for the military wing of the FIS. However, the decentralization of the movement, stemming in turn from internal dissensions and the nature of clandestine struggle, soon turn it into a series of splinter groups ensconced in stagnant compartments. Their weapons, which are gradually improving in quality and quantity, do not come from Sudan and Iran, as the official media maintains. Islamist fighters get them by attacking police stations, barracks, arms stores, and by taking the shotguns and rifles from the *mujahedin*, peasants, and mountain people. Individual or collective desertions—like those of the cadets in the military school in Cherchell—regularly swell their ranks and their arsenal. Although the resistance maquis spread throughout the country with the exception of the Sahara, repeated attacks on branches of banks and post offices add to the movement's resources and allow it to improve its infrastructure. Through information filtered through the press and the "Arab telephone," Algerians are now discovering to their amazement that their country is at war.

The growing *Lebanization* of the Algerian situation is a repeat with slight symphonic variations of the same score: the struggle against colonialism. Against the would-be "moderation" of the Armed Islamic Movement, which "only" executes the representatives of an "unholy government," a new movement, the Armed Islamic Group (GIA), proposes an out- and-out *jihad*, the preferred victims of which will be journalists, writers, poets, feminists, and intellectuals. Led in turn by Moh Leveilley (eliminated by the security forces), Abdelkader Layada (arrested when traveling through Morocco and handed over to the authorities in Algiers), Ja'far "Seifallah" the Afghan (killed in a recent clash with police in one of the districts of the capital), and, according to the latest news, by Saya Attia, the GIA demands immediately "distinguish themselves" by virtue of their ultimatum against foreigners, who were urged to leave Algeria in November 1993, and the subsequent murder of thirty-two foreigners, and moderate Islamist imams and women not wearing the *hijab*. The extension of the *haram* (what is forbidden) to every sphere of social and private life serves as a pretext to these righters of wrongs to infringe the basic norms of tolerance, in relation to women and coexistence with *dhimmis* or citizens of the other monotheist religions recognized by Islam. The moral and civic meltdown Algeria is experiencing has entered a new and bloodier spiral. Fratricidal struggles between the MIA and the GIA are throwing up dozens of casualties: although the GIA demand the "cleansing" of seventy MIA members, the responsiblity for the death of seven terrorists, whose corpses were discovered during my stay in Algeria, will be assigned by some sources to their internal wrangles and by others to their clandestine liquidation by secret para-police squads.

Harassed by the spreading of armed groups on the offensive in every area of society, Ali Kafi and General Nezzar intensify repression at the expense of dialogue: instead of the old, efficient strategy of divide and rule—deepening the differences that exist between the political and military wings of the FIS—they seem set on welding together all their enemies. The official belief, shared by many Democrats, that the

Islamists have isolated themselves from the people and that it is enough to reduce their bastions to reestablish order in the republic ignores the fact that in a conflict of the Algerian variety the might of the strongest is only superficial because material strength is powerless against a phantom: the messianic, justice-bearing ideals of the FIS rank and file. After freeing three French hostages who were in the hands of the GIA, there are enormous roundup operations in the poor districts of Algiers. At night tanks encircle Belcourt, Bab el-Oued, the Casbah, Kouba, and El Harrash, police in camouflage gear with high-powered rifles line up suspects, their hands above their heads, against the walls of the so-called Kabul mosque, burst into the homes of Afghan veterans, and carry out hundreds of arrests. Throughout the autumn, the *ninjas*, protected by an impressive array of helicopters and armored vehicles, scrutinize one by one the districts of Tagarinos, Eucaliptus, Baraki, and Climat de France, penetrate the hideouts of terrorists, impound clandestine documents and leaflets, and frisk presumed subversives before herding them into their vehicles and off to police stations and military centers. Television and other news media talk awkwardly about "clean-up operations," "pacifying measures," and "strengthening security" against "criminals," "pimps," and "antisocial elements." As the eyewitnesses of these operations testify, they bear a startling similarity to those of the War of Independence and French official communiqués. The country watches a replay of scenes from thirty-odd years ago, when Massu and Bigeard's men went through the Casbah with a "fine-tooth comb" looking for terrorists and men of violence. By a cruel irony of history, the tactic of the urban struggle of the Islamists replicates the FLN in its heroic heyday. Apparently a video made by members of the FIS records eloquent sequences from such raids. Its title should not come as a shock: it is quite simply *The Second Battle of Algiers*.

TERROR

My first contact with reality soon dispels hope of any kind of truce. The air hostesses on my flight to Algeria hand out daily papers with hefty doses of grim news. From the section headed "Terrorist Attacks Increase Throughout the Country" in *El Watan*, I focus in turn on an arson attack by thirty and armed hooded individuals on an Algerian department store car park in Hussein Dey; five policemen "executed" in Constantine; two seventy-three-year-olds, *mujaheddin* veterans from the War of Independence, and one other citizen, murdered in Blida; the parents of two policemen and a peasant, victims of terrorists in Chlef and Tisemilt; the governor of Larghouat prison shot to pieces in the marketplace; a correspondent for the daily paper *Alger Républicain* seriously wounded in Tiaret and another kidnapped in Bumerdès; sabotage and arson attacks in Bel Abbès and Relizan; and an army captain machine-gunned down a hundred meters from Algiers airport. This last act, carried out in a supposed identity check by so-called uniformed policemen, makes me, and no doubt many readers, intensely suspicious: how could these Islamists mount an operation of that nature on the most policed stretch of motorway in the whole country? The hypothesis, put around by someone, that they were real policemen is even more disturbing. The whole press points accusingly at the inexplicable absence of the state, its lack of a clear strategy, the passivity and aphasia of a political class confronted on all sides by the groups aspiring to take power. "Murder, sabotage, aggressions of all kinds are on the increase daily, creating an atmosphere of psychosis among the populace," writes the *Liberté* lead writer. "Algerians can't tolerate life under this degree of appalling rumour, hostages to a nebulous fortune that only manifests itself in death and intimidation."

Just after I touch down at the airport, someone with a longstanding knowledge of the realities of the country gives me the latest news: Ahmed Asela, the director of the School of Fine Arts, and his son Rabah have just been murdered. On the drive to my hotel, in a Spanish embassy car, I try to resurrect memories from previous visits. Algerian life apparently follows its normal course. The traffic has not improved. The blocks of working-class flats look even more rickety and dingy. *Ninjas* aim their weapons at vehicles at the checkpoints and flyovers on the motorway.

Fifteen, twenty, thirty years earlier I had stayed in the Aletti or the Oasis, hotels close to the port and the promenade. Present circumstances indicate a stay in the old Saint George, rebaptized as Al Jazair, on the hills overlooking Hydra and El Muradia. From my balcony I gaze at the beautiful bay of Algiers, the crisscross terraces of modern buildings and red-tiled, flat-roofed colonial villas, gardens, cypresses, minarets, benign shadows of satellite disks, boats at anchor waiting to unload, pigeons perched on the eaves of the neighboring house, their cooing all but lost in the muffled but continuous noise of the traffic.

"Oh Algeria, my capital!" A *chaabi* song, written by Abdelmadjid Meskoud and then adapted as a *rai* by Cheb Khaled, nostalgically reflects the author's feelings at the changes suffered by the city. Like François Villon's famous *Ballade*, it recalls what was but is no longer, what might have been but never was. I rest in my hotel, as the streets empty out in the twilight of Ramadan, and listen to the cassette participating in his melancholy feelings:

> Algiers! Algiers !
> Priceless capital
> You will live in my heart until Judgement Day.
> Unworthy people have harmed you
> Have mistreated you !
> Oh land of Sidi Abderrahman
> Home of the proud martyr and heroic saints
> City of Barbarossa and Sidi M'hamed, the one with
>   two tombs
> Tell me, you who listen to me, were has this
>   beauty's perfume gone?

> Tell me, what has become of the lives of its
>   children?

Abdelmadjid Meskoud looks in vain for the people who lived
there: he recognizes nobody in El Harrash, the people of
Hussein Dey and Kouba are scattered, El Hamma has been
ravaged, no trace of his parents remains in his beloved
Belcourt, Bab el-Oued and the Casbah have lost their flavor,
and neighborhoods are decaying as they have been abandoned and crowded by outsiders. The evocation of the fies-
tas, traditions, religious pilgrimages, songs, music, and poems
resound pathetically in these times of barbarism, intolerance,
and unhappiness. As I see for myself days later, the sanctuaries of Sidi Abderrahman in the top part of the Casbah and
of Sidi M'hamed, the patron saint of Belcourt, have been
profaned. The fanatical zeal of some enlightened souls set
fire to their tombs. Only a few faithful to their memory soak
up their grace or crouch waiting for alms from some charita-
ble passerby.

Might not the press perhaps exaggerate the climate of
panic or even partly whip it up? The attack on the television
reporter Hasan Benauda in the Casbah, hours after the murder of the director of the School of Fine Arts and his son,
fuels the most alarmist rumors and commentaries. "How
Much Longer?" "When Will the Blood and Tears End?" scream
the headlines in *Liberté*. The strategy of terror increasingly
points to one main objective: to force the population of the
different *wilayats* to collaborate under death threats in the
organization of the areas that the Islamists have already
dubbed *liberated zones*. This explains why the corpses of
various victims have been mutilated. . . . The terrorists
impose their law and kill whoever they want, wherever they
want, whenever they want. At the present moment, disillu-
sionment may be transformed into inactivity and resignation.
Algiers will become Kabul and Algeria, Afghanistan.

The following day, I accompany the correspondent of *El
País* and a delegate from the Spanish news agency EFE to the
burial of Ahmed Asela and his son. Several hundred people

assemble in the gardens of the School of Fine Art. Teachers, journalists, artists, and writers await the moment to walk past the catafalques. The atmosphere is somber. Some women are sobbing. What perverse logic willed this crime? What profit can be gained from the deaths of innocent people? The autonomous student committee from the School of Fine Arts distribute leaflets denouncing the "butchery," "the macabre melodrama that began with Boudiaf's murder," "the murderous bullets of the fundamentalists and the political-financial mafia": "Oh all powerful ones who art in heaven, get off your backsides, we're on the road to extinction!" As the bodies are about to be moved, clapping, shouting, and yoo-yoos resonate. At the Jaridi cemetery, the crowd watch the burial in a tense, anguished silence: the widow doesn't want funeral orations. Only one minister and a handful of representatives from the world of politics witness the ceremony thus emphasizing the isolation of intellectuals caught in a no-man's land. As journalists observe, visits here are becoming more and more frequent. The graves line up, Sarajevo-style, in sinister chronological order. Who will the next one be for? "Empty space in the cemetery is fast disappearing : the day will soon come, a friend of the deceased prophesies, when there won't be anywhere to bury us."

The wave of attacks is aimed at very precise targets: is it, as many people think, a "Pol Potian" strategy to finish off the intellectuals who have been infected by the West, a program of selective genocide? The list of the *liquidated* over the last few months points in that direction: but, as we shall see later, the victims encompass every layer of the population and the shots don't come from just one direction.

Since before 26 May 1993—the date of the yet-to-be-solved murder of my friend, the novelist Tahar Djaout, invited at my behest to Madrid a year earlier to a colloquium on North Africa organized by *Passages*—the editorial boards of both printed and visual news media have been receiving daily death threats by letter or telephone. The execution—sometimes beheading—of various editors and reporters soon created a panic-stricken psychosis. Fearing for their lives, writers who have most confronted the Islamists—especially in the francophone newspapers—use a pseudonym in their by-line, vary their working hours, avoid entering and leaving their houses at a predictable time, and continually change addresses until their nerves give way and they abandon the struggle and go into exile. "Life today is a constant back and forth from funerals to the airport to bid farewell to departing colleagues," one of those under threat confides to me. In the autumn, as the relentless struggle between the government and the Islamists intensifies, waves of fear extend into new areas. The Armed Islamist Group's (GIA) ultimatum to non-Muslim foreigners leads to a massive exodus. Some embassies and consulates shut up shop, others reduce their staff and send women and children back to their country of origin, move part of their offices to secure places, and transform premises and belongings into bunkers. Businessmen who do not give up the struggle leave their villas and flats and live and work from hotel rooms. Like diplomats, they reduce their time out to the absolute minimum necessary, frequently traveling with an armed escort in bullet-proof cars. "We are living in prison conditions," laments one of the few correspondents remaining in the country. Those who, because of their long residence in Algeria and addiction to the country, think they are immune to the epidemic pay with their lives for their error of judgment: a well-known bookseller and gallery owner of Spanish extraction and the owner of a video and cassette shop are shot dead at pointblank range in their workplaces in the heart of the capital. While the failed conference on national dialogue is being held, on the eve of the sacking of Ali Kafi from the High Committee of State and the appointment of Lamine Zeroual to the presidency of the Republic, a feeling of insecurity and powerlessness takes over the population submitted to frequent controls, alarmed by the ever more audacious strikes of the Islamists and savage retaliation by the forces of order. "Nobody lingers after work," writes one witness. 'No curfew is necessary, the streets empty out: fear achieves that. In this overcrowded capital solitude rules. In an emergency it is futile to ask for Help. Nobody will come. Too many calls for help have been excuses for ambushes . . . 3,000 dead? They say it could be five times that figure. How can one know precise figures with the censorship that exists?"

According to recent reports, more than a thousand Algerian intellectuals have sought political asylum in France. Most of them are teachers, doctors, lawyers, journalists, and writers educated as francophones. The creation of an Islamic state in Algeria would provoke an exodus of half a million people, according to Chris Hedges, correspondent for the *New York Times*. But not all the refugees belong to the *eradicating* tendency or are fleeing the MIA, the GIA, or the FIS. Many of the murders and summary executions are the work of *death squads* that, as in Colombia and other Latin American countries, are avenging the bullets that decimate the forces of order or prevent with their outrages any attempt at a political solution to the crisis. Several lawyers and members of the Algerian League for the Rights of Man, after denouncing the generalized practice of torture and the extrajudicial executions pinpointed by Amnesty International, have likewise received death threats: I know at least one of them who, according to a reliable source, was warned by a close relative that his name figured on a hit list and took the first plane to Paris.

In the brittle atmosphere pervading Algeria today, the activities of nonidentified commandos spread panic in circles sympathetic to the Islamists and are a normal part of everyday life. The mysterious Organization of Young Free Algerians has sworn to carry out the law of an eye for an eye on terrorists and kidnaps and murders relatives or friends of known members of the FIS. According to several reports, individuals clad in combat gear attack the homes of suspects during the curfew and the corpses of those captured turn up at dawn abandoned in the streets of the locality or, according to repeated press rumors, are taken from interrogation centers excavated half a century ago beneath French police stations wrapped in plastic bags for secret burial. During my stay in Algeria, a remarkably courageous lead writer did not hesitate to point at the hidden hand of the political-financial mafia behind these crimes "intent on permanently destabilising the country."

Who is killing who? In the paranoia gripping Algerians no one can respond with any certainty. If in a majority of cases a criminal hand is quite visible, in others doubts have yet to be dispelled. The Committee for the Truth about Tahar Djaout's murder has not made any progress at all: one of its members, a friend of the victim, was in turn cut down by a bullet and the others have been subject to constant threats. The popular television newscaster Abdelkadir Hirechi, eliminated at the beginning of Ramadan and whose death was at first laid at the door of the "fundamentalists," turned out to be an FIS member, according to a later communiqué from that organization. Since then, no group or faction has claimed responsibility for the crime.

The terrorism of the GIA and other armed groups—some people talk of the existence of 650 groups, made up of at least a dozen members!—now strikes out not only at defenseless women whose only crime is that they are mothers or wives of soldiers, gendarmes, or policemen, but also at religious personalities who preach tolerance and moderation. A seventeen-year-old girl was murdered in cold blood in Blida as a public example to those who refuse to wear the *hijab*, and the *sheikh* Buslimani paid with his life, according to statements from Hamas Mahfud Naha, the leader of the Islamist movement, for his refusal to promulgate a *fatwa* authorizing this kind of crime. In the last fourteen months, eight imams and *ulema* (Koranic experts) have been "executed" by the GIA, even inside their own mosques. Others of the faithful have been felled as they left prayers in the holy month of Ramadan. How can one explain this surge of madness and barbarism? Neither the religious creed nor a state that has any self-esteem can condone the savagery and brutality that is pushing Algeria toward the abyss.

In my hotel room I review the press before going to bed. Words from Salima Ghazali vividly sum up the feelings of many people I have come across: "In this vast cemetery that is Algeria, where our steps now take us from a closed tomb to an open one, first we buried ideas, dreams and words and then we enterred the executed bodies of men, women and children who lived with nothing and died for nothing."

OF SERMONS AND SATELLITE DISKS

How can one forge a clear idea of the present situation in Algeria if one's exclusive sources of information are frequently censored news bulletins from the local press or from foreign newspapers and press agencies? Don't these reports, based on events that are difficult to corroborate, only serve to exaggerate incidents that are already serious enough? By way of example: are there large areas of the country that are out of the army's control? Are hundreds of villages and towns in the hands of Islamic fundamentalists? Are the Aurès and Constantine undergoing a widespread "cleanup operation" supported by air power and artillery fire? Is the military high command holed up in bunkers and traveling by helicopter to their offices and meetings, as the *New York Times* affirmed on 25 January? Have 8,000 armed recruits deserted to the resistance as claimed by the same newspaper? Are whole areas of the capital, of Blida, and its periphery given over to the law of the Islamists after dusk? If food shortages and price increases provoked a mass insurrection, would the troops shoot at the populace? To what extent has the FIS infiltrated the officer class, the lower ranks, and regular troops? The black humor of some intellectuals has put this joke around: "In Algeria we already have a perfectly balanced rotation of our political executive. Government rule by day and FIS by night."

Any attempt to escape the paranoia of the ghetto where Europeans and intellectuals live under threat meets with numerous obstacles. In order to sidestep them I look for help from a trustworthy taxi driver, the generous friendship of Algerian colleagues, and a group of young Arabic writers who offer to escort me round the working-class districts considered to be bastions of Islamic fundamentalism. "Aren't you afraid?" the question repeatedly put to *El País* correspondent Ferrán Sales three months ago, as he left his office next to the Post Office and returned to his hotel, is no longer a question anyone bothers to ask: it would be as self-evident and obvious as the comment under a bright blue sky that the sun is shining. Will my ordinary clothing, incipient beard, and in particular my companions grant me a chameleon's invisibility or is that another of my illusions? At any rate, as I make my way round the Casbah, Bab El-Oued, or Belcourt no one seems to notice my insignificant presence. In fact, I don't know if I am the only European around or if there are others who are equally anonymous and undetectable.

A walk beneath the arcades on the seafront, known as Yusef Zirut, brings me back to my old hunting ground on Port Sa'id Square and then to Ernesto Che Guevara, and back to the city area I remember well: a scattering of office workers in suits and ties, a number of youngsters in jeans or sportswear, women silhouetted, their heads uncovered or "protected" by the *hijab* tied under their chins and imported into Algeria by the Islamists. Bearded men in their skullcaps and *kamis* or white overshirts are rarely seen: ever since the FIS was made illegal and the massive police round-ups, the majority of its supporters have shaved their beards and don the usual, more showy clothes worn in these districts. Port Sa'id Square, its benches filled with people out to make a quick dinar, unemployed or casual strollers, is a meeting point for the Nigerians and Senegalese who have just arrived at the nearby station. The large number of poor, curled up or asleep, is something new: the revolutionary Algeria of the sixties prided itself on having done away with them. Now they slip between cars at traffic lights asking drivers for money as they do in Madrid or London. The huge esplanade of the Martyrs' Square—given a new lease on life by kiosks and gardens—is as animated as ever. By one of the low brick walls a bearded old man wearing a skullcap and a white knee-length shirt quietly reads *Libért*, the French-language newspaper most radically opposed to Islamists.

We drive along a tree-lined avenue that crosses the lower part of Bab El-Oued. The visitor to the shabby *pied noir* quarter is still entranced by the brightly hued window shutters, the vivid, colorful washing hung to dry on the balconies, the noisy hubbub of its markets. The hidden economy, plugging the gaps in the official chain of supply, reveals the vitality and defense mechanisms of sectors of the population ignored by the state. As I will soon see for myself in the Casbah and Belcourt, the shops are well stocked, thanks to the *racket* or *trebando*, although prices are prohibitive for many pockets. The only queues line up in front of the stalls selling the oil, milk, and coffee so sought after in Ramadan. Police and soldiers have vanished since Lamine Zeroual took power: as I stroll through the areas described as troublesome I meet no patrols or armed militia. Should that be seen as a sign of confidence or cowardice, strength or weakness? Whatever the case, their absence creates a feeling of dead calm and lessens the tension in the packed streets, still marked by the impact of bullets from recent or long-ago confrontations.

How can the vision of this beguiling swarm of humanity be reconciled with the images of the October 1988 insurrection or the photographs of angry youths in conflict with the forces of law and order in May 1991, obeying the slogans of their religious leaders? After taking a quick look at the unfinished mosque, more like a hangar or building site, where Ali Belaj used to preach—the favorite imam of Bab El-Oued street kids—we leave it behind and walk down along Colonel Lotfi Boulevard, right into the heart of the district.

On my first sortie with the Algerian correspondent of the EFE press agency, I visit Sidi Abderrahman's profaned mausoleum and, as cautious as ever, get myself a candle blessed with his grace, then cross the Casbah along Abderrahman Arbadyi Street to the old synagogue that has been converted into a mosque. Still following my guide, I cut down the steps of an alley to the broader thoroughfare of Arezki Buzrina and rediscover to my delight the Turkish mosque of Ketshuwa, adapted for Catholic services by the French who turned it into a cathedral, which was then restored to its previous state as a mosque after independence and the sudden disappearance of its flock. Its hybrid architecture reflects a turbulent history and calls for a leisurely visit, but my companion brings me back to the harsh realities of the present by pointing out the spot where forty-eight hours earlier the television journalist Hasan Benauda had fallen seriously wounded. The route through the districts of Bab El-Oued and the Casbah is hardly for tourists: as I write these lines, the radio announces the murder of an editor working on the official daily paper, *El Moudjahid*.

Once again, accompanied by a trio of young writers, I go to areas where twenty years ago I walked without a care, and which are now the seedbed of Islamic Front militants. The Casbah, singled out by Le Corbusier as a "masterpiece of urban architecture," preserves the charm and fascination of old buildings on the verge of collapse, despite the lack of adequate sanitation and the suffocating crowding of its inhabitants. As I lose myself in the labyrinthine alleyways of the old Turkish citadel, gaze down on the genial improvisation of layer upon layer of terraces where women hang out their washing, and imitate the people walking up and down the steep steps my heady excitment has to be the most beautiful memory of my stay in Algiers. Nevertheless, after the initial moment of being dazzled by a prismatic world whose criss-cross, winding alleys make me feel I am in the medinas of Fez or Tangiers, the running sores of the general crisis in the country stand out like patches of grease gleaming on water. Most hand-crafted and nationally produced goods have disappeared: the public buys up leftovers from European industry and clothes made in Korea, China, and Taiwan. Rubbish and waste pile up outside dingy gaping holes and foul-smelling drains. Kids play in unhealthy spots, in flight from the tensions and unbearable promiscuity of their homes. The picture is not very different from that of the inner cities of other Arab and non-Arab cities, but here the negligence of the state and autarky of the population combine in a way that explains the success of the Islamists. Everything is organized along autonomous channels, behind the backs of the official authorities. Ever since the earthquake of 1989, which shook and fissured the foundations of several buildings in the Casbah, the FIS openly or secretly organizes social activity in the area. Though I can't see any sign of them, are there also secret police making up for the absence of official police ever since last year's nighttime roundups? Nobody is willing or able to answer my question, or perhaps no one knows the answer. The initiatives of this hidden presence spread, as in Kouba or El Harrash, where the bust of Emir Abdelkader—symbol of the heroic Algerian resistance to the French colonial invasion—was pulled from its pedestal in the middle of the park by rivals to the iconoclasts without provoking a reaction from the municipal authorities. FIS slogans festoon the walls of the capital's working-class districts and outskirts: in the present situation no local worthy bothers to get them removed.

However, the radical groups' program for the re-Islamization of society has registered a significant failure in the matter of satellite disks. A large number of buildings display them even in the most down-at-heel areas of the Casbah, either the result of collective subscriptions or through ingenious, home-made connections with the nearest disk. As the only consolation or distraction from the closed horizons of their world, the locals enjoy a surfeit of deceitful, deadening images from the would-be orgy of European consumerism, the Great World Market of mass-produced sex and violence. The Casbah isn't alone in this: the phenomenon is repeated in Bab El-Oued, Belcourt, El-Harrash, Salambier, and Climat de France (the housing estate subsidized by Ferdinand Pouillon now nicknamed by its inhabitants as *Climat de sou(s)ffrance* [an untranslatable pun: a climate of suffering and under-France]) because of the oppressive atmosphere and runaway decay. In spite of FIS campaigns against the pornography and pulp television of Spanish Channel 5 and French Channel +, satellite disks have spread as rapidly as mosques. Punitive incursions make no impact: after the militants have made their foray, locals soon reestablish their connection to the main cable. Sermons are no match for the plague of satellite disks. Frequently the youths who call passionately for setting up an Islamic state and the strict application of the *shari'a* assuage their frustration and impatience by taking a peek at the hated, disturbing, unattainable universe on the opposite shore of the Mediterranean.

The collective neurosis affecting Algeria is the result of a combination of insoluble contradictions: the same people who express heartfelt aversion to the corruption and aggression of the West would grasp, if they could, the first opportunity to emigrate to France. Quite unconsciously, they imitate the schizophrenia of FLN party bosses who self-righteously pontificate about the arrogance and terrible legacy of French imperialism and then take off with their mistresses for weekend sprees in Paris, to the luxury hotels and shops of the Champs Elysées and Faubourg de Saint Honoré.

Does a linguistic barrier separate two Algerias, one that is backward, traditional, and Arabic-speaking and one that is open, progressive, and French-speaking? The way that some "democrats" or spokespersons for the so-called "French Party" present the situation confuses rather than clarifies this duality. It is true that, during the era of Ben Bella and Boumedien, Arabic speakers felt excluded from the administration and state monopolies where the various elements of the financial-political mafia were amassing huge fortunes. The socialistic modernity of the FLN scorned the imams and Arabic teachers or treated them with the same paternalistic condescension as the colonizers. French was—and, to a lesser extent, continues to be—the language of government, industry, and business, of the political élites who ruled and continue to rule the country. The campaign of compulsory Arabization during the seventies and the era of Chadli Bendjedid did not bear the desired fruit: on the contrary, it led to endless educational disasters, discredited state schools, and provoked the exodus of failed examination candidates and semiliterates to Islamic schools and mosques. The gap between the dialect spoken by the people—I shall leave for the time being the problem of Berber language and identity—and standard, modernized Arabic, spread by press and television, largely explains this failure: the conformist, fossilized, insipid, neutral language used in written or broadcast news bulletins, rehearsed ad nauseam day after day is in the end rejected by listeners and readers who are bored by clichés and commonplaces bearing no relation to the mother tongue they speak. As a result of an arbitrary and inept Arabization, the number of students able to handle correctly either French or Arabic was drastically reduced: the level of education declined and modest improvements in Arabic were not compensated for by the general falloff of the use of French. French speakers accused the imams and teachers brought in from the Near East of incompetence and took advantage of the political liberation flowing from the events of October 1988 to get their own back. On an equal footing with Arabic in the real testing ground of the marketplace, French won an outright victory, according to Tahar Djaout: the circulation of French-language newspapers was three times that of those published in the national language. In fact, such success was ephemeral and limited to a well-defined sector: social groups who had benefited from almost three decades of single-party rule and the political minorities and lay intellectuals who supported a multiparty democracy, as Ferhat Abbas had forty years earlier. The efforts of a genial writer like Kateb Yacine to promote the mother tongue to unleash, through theater plays in dialect, the daily experiences of the people and feelings usually proscribed by the wooden language of officialdom, opened the way for the satirical work of Sliman Benaissa and the successful adaptation of the orality of the *halqa* by the recently murdered director from Oran, Abdelkadir Alloula. But the freeing of *darija*, the ordinary Arabic used by millions of non-Berber Algerians, despite the enriching potential, comes up against both the elitism of French speakers and the *normalizing* project of the Islamists.

The opinions of some of my Arabic informants on the present situation and its probable evolution differ from those one usually hears expressed in France by novelists and writers under attack from the FIS. Although they all condemn the attacks and intimidation suffered by their colleagues, they think, as one confided to me, that they are only "explaining the truth about Algeria to the French in French." Their concerns, an FIS supporter told me in Paris, are not those of the majority of other Algerians: "The shock-waves hitting us have suddenly made them feel strangers in their own land and this discovery, added to their fear, is forcing them into exile." "Wasn't it the same in Russia in 1919 or Germany in 1933?" "Algeria isn't Russia or Germany. We are still struggling against the legacy of colonialism!" "Are terrorist methods and retrograde practices part of this struggle?" My interlocutor doesn't want to commit himself and prefers to emphasize, by way of justification, the living conditions of the Algerian people and the cultural aggression suffered by his fellow countrymen. We agree only on one thing: the violent death of an unemployed youth in Bab El-Oued and Belcourt is no less horrific and unacceptable than that of a writer.

When I read in a clandestine pamphlet that "the members of the *hizb fransi* (French Party) must follow the example of the *pieds noirs* and head for their real fatherland," this desire to have a clean-out brings to mind other unhappy periods in Spanish history. Like almost all the countries of the Mediterranean, Algeria is surely the result of a mixture of races and a fertile compenetration of cultures. In the choice between a reductive, homogenizing conception, condemned to monologue and one that is receptive, plural, and open to dialogue, both the Spanish and Arab experiences demonstrate that the victory of the former heralds a cultural wasteland and the sterile rule of dogmatism. "We must integrate within our history, with its multiple contradictions, the hundred and thirty years of French presence," writes the historian Mohammed Harbi. "To try to restore the ancient order of things to its pristine purity is futile."

Those of us who have experienced the reality of *ethnic cleansing* in Bosnia and the sinister role played by Serbian purifiers and myth makers in the destruction of that cultural inheritance and historical substrata can only endorse his words. Algeria is not a uniform entity: it has always been rich and varied and will either be a land for all its children or will be lost to feuding sects in an endless civil war.

MUSICAL CHAIRS

On the eve of my departure, I decide to spend a few hours in Blida. Everybody had warned me off. According to the democratic opposition's publications, "The fundamentalists are in complete control": "Going round Blida is like drifting into a nightmare. The 'city of roses' is a shadow of its former self. Anguish and fear are in everyone's eyes." (*El Watan*, 3 August, 1994). Other press agencies maintain that the road to Chrea, on the way to the mountains, is in the hands of Islamists and that "bands of fanatics are imposing their law on the industrial estate of Ulad Yaich." The fifty-kilometer journey from the capital goes quite smoothly: no checkpoints or police presence. Only on the road into Blida, by a cross-roads near the marketplace, do a tank and several armed soldiers watch the flow of traffic. I accompany my writer friends on a walk along the main avenue with its faded colonial villas covered and almost asphyxiated by bougainvillea, past the square with the town hall, palm trees, and central kiosk, down streets bustling because of 'Id el Fitr, the imminent end to the fasting of Ramadan. Of the women I come across only three are not wearing the *hijab*; women's hairdressers and beauty salons have been closed; newspaper stands display no publications in French; nor do I notice shops selling or renting out videocassetes. I am not able to confirm with my own eyes reports that women's baths have been banned (!) or that bus companies must separate the sexes in their vehicles. For some weeks, gangs of adolescents recruited by the GIA have apparently been "convincing" inhabitants to do without television and radio, spreading panic in schools to the point of enforcing orthodox clothing on students and female schoolteachers. The press in Algiers talks of countless physical attacks and the murder of a young *mutabarraha* (provocative woman) who refused to accept the state of *muhsana* ("protection" afforded by modest dress and head-scarf). My attempts to investigate the facts were a failure.

Neither in Blida nor anywhere else in Algeria will people confide in strangers and even less so in foreigners. The law of silence seals all lips.

"Don't stay here very long, it could be dangerous for you," begged one of my companions.

Resigned, I follow his advice, with the frustrating impression that I have only half achieved my goal: that of examining at firsthand the strange cohabitation that exists in several places in Algeria between the state and Islamists, a prefiguration of a possible accord that could perhaps be negotiated later. The strong, well-equipped army presence in Blida and other points in the Mitidja remain confined to barracks, leaving the economic, social, and religious organization of the city to the FIS. After the failure of the massive roundups and the policies of General Khaled Nezzar—which only went to show how easily the Islamists recruit new militants from the endless reserves of unemployed youths to replace those in prison—the new president, Lamine Zeroual, is opting to cool the situation and to prepare the terrain for an indispensable national dialogue with his interlocutors in the FIS.

The president's speech on 7 February is in fact the first really serious attempt to negotiate the end to the civil war tearing Algeria apart. His conviction that the "many-sided crisis" in the country is that of "a society aspiring to radical change" and that this change "must mean a real, complete break, involving the whole of society, the forces behind cultural, political, social and economic life," leads him to promote dialogue "as the basis for political action" until he has created the necessary conditions for a return to the electoral process: to free elections by the people of its representatives, with no manipulation or pressure of any kind. Does that mean things have to return to the starting point of the coup of January 1992 without calling to account those who were behind that decision as the FIS demanded? Or is the proposal to turn to a clean page and forget the mistakes committed on both sides? Although Zeroual is not explicit in that respect, his political program leans toward the second option. At any rate, his conviction that a simple policy of law and order cannot get the country out of the mire forces him to propose a way out through agreement with all the parties "without exception." Just before his investiture in his post, Zeroual had spoken in terms very similar to Boudiaf, of the need to restore a moral sense to public life, and had denounced the excrescence of a "parasitic ideology"; the undermining activities of "interest groups in several decision-making centers in the economy, administration and other key points of the State." The more than transparent allusion to the destabilizing intervention of the political financial mafia as well as the hand offered to the FIS, drawing a line between it and the armed extremist groups, allows one to catch a glimmer of hope, a possible end to this dark tunnel.

Lamine Zeroual clearly belongs to the sector of the army that acted for two decades in the belief that it was working for progress and the modernization of Algeria until it discovered with Chadli Bendjedid that the FLN's monopoly of political life had fostered only nepotism and bribery, the advent of a ubiquitous caste that had literally taken over the state. A bitter awakening, shared by so many self-denying militants who, after dedicating their lives to the service of the Revolution, suddenly realised the extent to which they had been swindled. Although some army leaders, close to the financial oligarchy and clinging to their privileges, accepted scrupulously the order to shoot against the people in October 1988, this decision upset honest chiefs and officers—not to mention the ordinary troops, flung head-over-heels into fratricidal repression—forcing them to reexamine their role in relation to the state and society as a whole. The division between those defending the obliteration of the FIS—taught a lesson by what happened to their colleagues in Iran after the fall of the shah—and the supporters of negotiations with Madani and Belhaj has deepened recently within the military leadership that coopted Zeroual into the presidency of the Republic. Although right in the front line after the breakup of the FLN and the inexplicable silence of most leaders of the democratic opposition, the army—heir to all those fighters who dreamed of an industrialized Algeria, improvements to rural life, and the eradication of illiteracy—would be very reluctant to embark on another coup d'état. Recent experience in other countries has shown how putting tanks on the street without a viable, popular program does not resolve problems but rather makes them worse.

An excellent analysis by Nureddin Khelassi in the Algerian weekly *La Nation* (3 September 1994) summed up the five fronts on which the new president must fight: negotiate the prickly dialogue with the FIS; lead the offensive against the extremist armed groups; reach a feasible accord with the International Monetary Fund (IMF); create a forum for discussion with the scattered democratic opposition; and break definitively with the corrupt practices of an ubiquitous, subterranean clique. The game that Zeroual must play reminds me of the game of musical chairs in which each participant runs the risk of being out if they do not react quickly and skillfully. But the danger for Algerian players does not come merely from the speed and cunning of their rivals but from within their own camp: each factor in the political equation is subject to real tensions and inner conflicts, which reflect the centrifugal tendencies within the country's old tribal structure, so evident in Emir Abdelkadir's struggle against the French invasion and the fragmentation and rivalry between the *wilayats* during the war of liberation.

The first problem for the new president is thus the difference of opinion within the army that put him into power: according to reliable sources, the rank and file and middle ranks reflect different currents within the society, from Islamist sympathizers to supporters of a lay military regime similar to the one created by Ataturk in Turkey seventy years ago. Zeroual's government program no doubt meets with resistance from the quartet of generals who appointed him. The questions asked in the press—is he free to act independently or must he seek the backing of the people really in control?—have yet to be answered clearly. As the commentator in *Le Matin* observes, "As long as Zeroual cannot get a cross-section in the army to come to decide in his favor, his task of advancing a political solution through reaching a compromise with the FIS can only mature at the same rhythm as that correlation grows." If his aims and strategy are evident, his ability to act is not. Each day that goes by, each bitter round of deaths erode his credibility and the hopes of those who want to break out of the nightmare.

The goodwill gesture of freeing two well-known Islamist leaders is not enough: an untrammeled dialogue with the FIS must proceed with Madani and Belhaj. That means they must immediately be released from jail and there time must be allowed to summon the *majlis ash-shura* (the Consultative Assembly) before the negotiating process is started. A return to the situation existing before June 1991 would encounter a new set of difficult circumstances. Terrorism, repression, and the blood spilled on both sides has led to traumas and open wounds that are not easily healed. On the other hand, because of the "neutralizing" of the leading group—at present in prison, in hiding, or in exile—the FIS today encompasses a range of factions and groups claiming to act in the name of Islamic principles and norms, but which are now divided among themselves by ferocious personal and political rivalries: the GIA now accuse historical leaders of opportunism, betrayal, and of diluting their program for the strict application of the *shari'a*. Simultaneously, the fear of many in the military—shared by Said Saadi's Alliance for Culture and Democracy and the ex-Communists—that the freeing of Abbassi Madani will be the first step in his elevation to the presidency of the state within a fairly short period, also represents a threat to the fragile process of negotiation. Equally, participation by the legal Islamist movements, Hamas and En-Nahda, would facilitate dialogue and introduce a reasonable, moderating element.

The position of the lay political parties is an alarming example of aphasia, paralysis, and division. Although the degeneration of the FLN machine gathers apace—the General Union of Algerian Workers (UGTA) has just split away—the main opposition movement, the Front of Socialist Forces (FFS) remains inexplicably silent before the wave of murders of intellectuals and the terrorism of Islamist armed

groups and squads of parallel police. In statements to a
Spanish newspaper, its old historical leader, Ait Ahmed, has
explained that his new exile in Europe came about because
he was afraid of meeting the same fate as Boudiaf. "I don't
want to be the second on the list," he said. But what about
his rank and file? Is it in any way open to them to take refuge
in France or Switzerland? By their silence and inaction—
what is Ben Bella saying or doing at this critical moment?—
the democratic movements, with the exception of Said Saadi'
and Hachemi Cherif's Ettahadi, the only ones present in these
dramatic times for the future of Algeria, run the risk of picking up the tab for any eventual compromise between the
government and the FIS. The women's demonstration on 8
March, International Women's Day, at the entrance to the Ibn
Khaldun cinema, did not enjoy the support of the parties and,
according to the press, the march against terrorism and "dialogue with the terrorists" was backed only by the two groups
just mentioned. This inability to create a front coupled with
the outright rejection of any negotiating initiative vis-à-vis the
party that got the majority of its citizens' votes reflects an
impoverished vision of the realities of Algeria. The exclusion
of the FIS from its vision of society is neither democratic nor
viable. Democracy cannot prosper in the shadow of tanks
like some besieged fortress, nor do present trends favor the
establishing of an Ataturk-style regime. Firm negotiations
by the army with every ploy it can muster does not imply
surrender. The popular perception of the FIS is that of a
Messianic alternative never sullied by the holding of power;
on the other hand, persecution and martyrology intensify the
glow of the saviors' halo: to force them to submit to the acid
test of presiding over an unwieldy economic crisis would
force them down from their idealized preacher's pulpit. Last
but not least, though it may allow them to win in theory, the
extremists' terror and violence will in no sense enable them
to convince those who remain lukewarm. In elections free
from pressurizing and manipulation like the ones promised
by Zeroual, I have reason to believe that they would receive
less votes than they would have three years ago. Many

Algerians can no longer accept such intolerance or such brutal, cursory methods of exacting justice.

There remains the fourth, most elusive player: *the political-
financial mafia.* Supposedly sidelined by the blows of recent
years, it constantly reappears like the hydra of Lerna: no
Hercules has yet decapitated at a stroke its seven heads. The
privatization of Algeria's industrial base and the ruinous state
companies, as in the countries of eastern Europe, is the center of its insatiable desire. The old bosses of the nationalized
companies are fighting among themselves to appropriate
them. It takes one *nomenklatura* to recognise another and its
survival depends on destabilization.

A more complete analysis of the crossroads facing Algeria
would have to include the problem of the Kabylia and the
other Berber minorities—the Chouis and Mozabites—as well
as the position of women, deprived, after their courageous
participation in the War of Independence, of all freedom of
opinion, expression, and conscience: their isolation, pathetically exposed on 8 March, shows how they are excluded
from all the political programs and visions of future society.
Since 1984 women have been subjected to a Family Code that
is more restrictive than in Tunisia and Morocco, and they are
sacrificial victims of insults and aggression: a quick glance at
the correspondence from rejected or divorced women in
Algérie Hebdo reveals more about their situation than fallacious statistics from ministries and propaganda leaflets from
those with no right to speak on their behalf.

What will happen to Algeria in the coming months and
years? To the hypotheses put forward by one of the best
specialists in the area, the sociologist Sami Nair (the Iranian
way: victory for the Islamists; the Chilean way: an army coup
d'état; the Republican way: power-sharing between the military, the FIS, and the democratic forces), I would add another
that is equally possible and even more disturbing: disintegration into rival gangs and clans, a Lebanese-style civil war, the
spreading of *iba* (anarchy). Or a social explosion following
an intolerable set of price increases imposed during negotiations with the IMF. We should not forget this: interest on the

debt in 1994 amounts to $9 million although predicted income from the sales of hydrocarbons does not even begin to reach this figure. Against such a bleak panorama, of underground war, social decay and economic ruin, what margin for maneuver does Zeroual have? The reply to this question cannot and must not be deferred.

Battered by the whirlwind sweeping across Algeria, citizens who aspire modestly to live without being terrorized or threatened find themselves in the position of the students in the School of Fine Arts after their director's murder: like a species on the verge of extinction.

When will the future start? Where does hope begin?

In the meantime, we should pause to listen to the inimitable words of the poet Tahar Djaout:

> Silence is death
> and if you say nothing
> you die,
> and if you speak
> you die.
> so speak and die.

NEITHER PEACE

NOR WAR:

THE WEST BANK AND

GAZA

THE GAZA POWDER KEG

From the balcony of the Tel Aviv Ramada, at dusk the visitor surveys a scrupulously clean beach lined by four-star hotels where the young and not so young, in track suits or other sporting gear play volleyball, jog, or test their physical stamina with an eye to an eventual marathon. The view is that of any European or American coastal city with its pools for swimmers, snack bars, and flags flapping in the sea breeze. The sun is sinking fast and the twilight softens and diffuses surfaces and colors theatrically in keeping with the serenity of the moment.

Do the citizens and tourists who make up this scene of carefree leisure know the reality of life for the inhabitants of the Gaza Strip that is barely an hour's ride away along the modern network of roads linking Israel's cities and farms? State television and the ubiquitous, ever-present U.S. channels send out images of enraged Palestinian demonstrators or angry members of some kibbutz as a result of the latest daily incident, the inevitable residue, according to the CNN broadcaster, of the "already extinguished flame of the *intifada.*" Israelis and Palestinians are negotiating an arduous peace process and the attention of the media now focuses on the regular meetings of Rabin and Peres with Arafat. The war is over, they tell us, and Gaza is a narrow coastal strip where the PLO puts its negotiating good faith to the test in the framework of the conferred autonomy.

Nevertheless, the illusion created by the Washington Declaration of Principles and the Oslo Accords swiftly fades before the harsh reality of the facts. Gaza has yet to embody a pilot project: it is, and continues to be, an unpredictable, potential powder keg.

The frontier post of Erez contains all the elements of this explosive situation. Six years ago when I passed through with my colleagues from the television crew for the series

Alquibla, the Israeli military police submitted us to a long wait before authorizing our entry. Today, their control and inspection posts seem to have been strengthened but the taxi with an Israeli license tag in which I am traveling slips down one of the routes marked out for cars without anyone asking for my passport or enquiring as to the reasons for my visit to a seventy-kilometer-long by twenty- to thirty-wide ghetto, where more than eight hundred thousand inhabitants are cooped up. I quickly cross no-man's-land, pass through the much more modest, poorer checkpoint belonging to the National Palestine Authority, and reach the battered service station where another taxi with a white Gaza license plate awaits me.

A deceptive impression of normality. If the name of Erez symbolizes in the press one of the habitual meeting points of Israeli and Palestinian leaders, it is equally a frequent scenario of confrontations. On 17 July 1994, just after Arafat was installed in Gaza, the thousands of workers who arrive daily at the border control post to work in Israel mutinied, exasperated by the long wait and the bureaucratic hassles: the Palestinian police intervened and twelve hours of crossfire led to two dead and more than a hundred Palestinians wounded; the crowd, apparently spurred on by Hamas (the Islamic Resistance Movement), burned 152 buses of the already sparse Gaza fleet; seventeen Israeli soldiers were injured and wounded and, as a result, the Strip was closed off for several days. Both sides accused the other of provocation and no impartial enquiry established the truth of the matter or who was responsible. A few days before I arrived, another so-called "provocation" by the Palestinian police ended with a full-scale assault by Tsahal (the Israeli army) on a house in a neighboring village where the "aggressors" had taken refuge: the latter were driven out and the *Jerusalem Post*—spokesman for the hard-line Israeli right—accused them of being Hamas agents who had infiltrated the ranks of Arafat's new police.

In fact, these incidents are a regular occurrence and never rate a mention in the press: in the present phase of the confrontation the wounded are no longer news. People living in

the frontier area talk of nightly shootouts and youths hospi-
talized. At night, the Israelis shoot at everything that moves.

The first glimpse of the districts of Beit Hanun, Jabalya,
and Gaza reveals a dirty, devastated urban expanse: water-
logged roadways, potholes stretching across the asphalt like
smallpox sores; ruined or burned-out buildings, empty, hollow eyesockets and open jaws; immense sewers carrying all
manner of refuse and detritus; walls covered in slogans;
clapped-out carts pushed by children.

In Beit Hanun I recognize the barbed-wire fence of the old
security headquarters of Tsahal where the Israeli journalist Ari
Shavit spent his military service and about which he wrote a
beautiful, moving account of the generalized use of torture.
The grey, apparently anodyne building, still surrounded by
the paraphernalia of security and vigilance, is now home to
the new Palestinian police, but I don't know whether its cells
are still filled with Hamas and Islamic Jihad activists.

To drive through the inner city of Gaza, one needs an
expert driver. Sami, recommended by *El País*'s Middle East
correspondent, twists and turns through interminable mud-
flats, waterlogged areas, and districts lacking even the most
basic infrastructure, a result of the tenfold increase in the
number of inhabitants over the last forty-five years and the
brutal Israeli occupation that has yet to end.

Before the *nakba* or disaster of 1948, the Gaza Strip had
around ninety thousand inhabitants. The first Israeli-
Palestinian war provoked the flight and settlement in the territory of more than two hundred thousand people. The
refugees were lodged in improvized camps with the help of
UNRWA (the UN Relief and Works Agency for Palestinian
Refugees): huts and hovels, without any basic services, were
set up as provisional. Those displaced in 1948 refused to be
resettled in more acceptable conditions, expecting soon to be
returned to the homes they had abandoned in Jaffa, Haifa, St.
John of Acre, or any of the four hundred villages that were
gradually swept off the map to establish new kibbutzim on
their ruins. Just like Spanish Jews and Muslims of the diaspora,
they lovingly retained the keys and title deeds to their houses

and orchards that now only exist in their memories and dreams. Attempts by UNRWA to build anything solid were rejected by the refugees, who clung to the unreality of memory. In the fifties, Gaza suffered harshly from the incursions of Tsahal and the brief Israeli occupation of 1956 during the Anglo-French military expedition against Nasser. After the political fiasco of the operation—the United States replaced England and France as the hegemonic power of the region— the enclave became the seedbed for the future *fedayeen*. Arafat, Abu Jihad, and so on—those who would soon be leaders of Al Fatah and the PLO—grew up and were forged in these years in the refugee camps of Gaza. The second disaster of 1967, and subsequent Israeli occupation, marked a new period of Palestinian resistance and harrassment. For a period of four years, Ariel Sharom's special units imposed a curfew, besieged and stifled the areas of conflict, carried out massive roundups, and applied collective punishment until *order was imposed.* . . . From 1971 to the beginning of the *intifada*, the Gaza territory experienced a precarious peace under the boot of the occupying force while Israeli settlements, especially around Rafah, multiplied and expanded.

The "war of stones" opens up a new phase in the long, violent, and exhausting confrontation. When I went to shoot a film on the *intifada*, seven of the eight large refugee camps were subject to martial law and were hermetically cordoned off, the Israeli army had also sealed off the center of the city, and the whole territory was a desolate panorama of repression, suffering, and misery.

Vehicles venture gingerly in most of the urban area along flooded paths where every so often truck tires stick out, like coral reefs, which youths set on fire during the *intifada*, or battered, mangy rubbish containers. Yet trade is picking up, albeit timidly: as we near the center, garages, repair shops, grocers, and fruit stalls spring up, even furniture stores with the loathsome armchairs that on another occasion I dubbed Louis XXVI, popularized by the tear-jerking serials on Egyptian TV. However, few Gazans have the means to acquire them and rest thereon their opulent buttocks.

The main commercial thoroughfare, the avenue of Omar al Mokhtar, is unrecognizable to anyone who saw it six years ago. Its bazaars and shops were closed, barriers and barbed wire blocked sidestreets, and several jeep-loads of Tsahal soldiers armed to the teeth prevented my friends and myself from proceeding by flourishing their threatening M-16s. Today, the roadway is packed with cars and the crowd swarms on the pavement, dodges through the traffic, and inspects and bargains over the wares in the bazaars. In the square, hundreds of banners with the printed photos of murdered PLO leaders flutter in the breeze. The Arab Bank and Bank of Palestine have opened their doors and the mosque, a beautiful building, welcomes the faithful with its walls covered in calls to holy war.

I leave till later the coastal area where the Palestine National Authority is based and follow the call of memory: Shatti, the only refugee camp I was able to slip into in 1988 under extremely harsh circumstances. The wall surrounding it has been demolished and I freely enter its labyrinth of alleyways between modest dwellings made from wooden boards and tin roofs. From the hill overlooking the coast, I gaze down on a variegated scenario of small flags, television aerials, boilers, and containers converted into makeshift water tanks. There are no drains, no sewers. Wastepipes pour their filth into narrow channels which, thanks to the slope, in turn spill out on the beach. The washing hanging out over shacks and rooms is the best indication of a high birth rate: the underwear and garments on display come in all sizes and range from nappies for the newly born to track suits for fifteen- or sixteen-year old girls and boys. I count up and reckon on an average family of five or six. When I look seaward, I spot a protective barrier of rocks and a rubbish-strewn beach where dozens of children are playing. A boy in swimming trunks and shirt braves the waves and tries to fish with a windswept net. To the right, on the road to Gaza, several buildings are under construction and two steamrollers are hard at work flattening out a future seafront promenade.

As I return to my departure point, a forty-year-old man, wearing the Palestinian black-and-white-checked *kaffiyeh*, chats with an older man—I soon discover it is his father— by the entrance to a house. After greeting me and finding out I speak Arabic, he invites me to sit down and have a coffee.

"Things haven't changed here," he tells me. "There's neither hope nor future. If I could leave for another country, I'd go straightaway. Before we were trapped in a cage for weeks on end, unable to get out. Now the cage has got bigger, but we're still imprisoned."

My next visit was to the old camp of Yabaliya, the biggest and most populated in Gaza and the one that withstood and suffered the most during the *intifada*. Generally it looks less depressing than Shatti. It has two-or three-story buildings, some of which are whitewashed. The walls of dwellings sometimes bear simple slogans with the Palestinian flag, the Dome on the Rock flanked by two machine guns, a dove with a black-and-white *kaffiyeh* breaking through the bars of its cell and flying off to freedom. On the sandy bed of a stream there is a collective taxi rank, carts pulled by donkeys or jennies, flocks of sheep, and a marketplace overflowing with fruit and vegetables. Above the roofs, amid electric cables, television aerials, and water tanks, the old Tsahal lookout post peers down like a threatening periscope or nosey giraffe. Two youths play dominoes on a cardboard box. A small monument with a stone commemorates those fallen in the *intifada*.

I settle down with Sami on the pavement of a small café opposite the UNRWA offices. From there customers can observe at their leisure what was the Israeli barracks with its wire fences, gates, and watch-posts. The fear and anxiety that reigned over Yabalya for years have gone. But, as I shall see during my stay, the district secretes visible frustration, stoked by anger and resentment against a bitter peace.

The owner of the café and his friend immediately identify my North African dialect. They worked for five years in Algeria and Morocco and nostalgically recall their happy stay in Casablanca.

"There is no future for the youth of Gaza. I have a quali-
fication in biochemistry and look at me: barely surviving as a
café owner."

His friend asks me if I know Cheb Khaled and we evoke
his songs and those by other stars of *rai*.

Before I bid farewell, the owner points to a rusty container
full of earth, with holes that serve to drain it, protected by a
metal gauze from the wind or children's vandalism, a kind of
cage where a spindly tree prospers or, rather, agonizes
despite the care bestowed on it.

"Photograph that," he tells me, "and you'll have a concrete
image of the reality of the Palestinian National Authority."

ARAFAT IN THE LOBSTER POT

On my previous visit to Gaza, the Israeli military barred our way to the southern half: their assault rifles turned us back a few kilometers from Deir el Balah. The road has been open since the *intifada* ended: my taxi zigzags between the oil drums and cement blocks of the benign or indolent Palestinian police checkpoint. The old, ill-treated central roadway cuts straight through orchards and orange groves. The plastic sheeting over *tempranal* grapes and force-farmed beds gleams in the sun. At the crossroads leading to the nineteen settlements, Tsahal's security posts on hilltops protected by sandbags oversee the traffic barely a hundred meters from those of their old enemy. This immediacy unwanted by either side often provokes incidents and victims: Palestinians accuse the Israelis of being trigger-happy and the latter denounce armed commando raids by Hamas. The signposts to Netzarim, Katif, and Neveh Dgalim are written in Hebrew and English. Khan Yunis seems to be surrounded by Jewish settlements and the impression of a siege intensifies in Rafah.

The southern capital presents an appearance of normality: steaming kebabs, shops well stocked, fruit stalls with enormous bunches of bananas, mysterious import-export companies. After taking a look at the wretched slum town of Sheikh el 'Id packed with thousands of refugees from 1948 and their offspring, we drive along the new, well-maintained side roads, toward the large settlements near the Egyptian frontier and contemplate the harsh reality of the injustice imposed by the victors.

The impregnable zone of Gush Katif shelters an enormous military base guarded by barbed-wire fences and electric gates. Spread over an area of two or three kilometers, its installations are modern and state of the art: hangars, barracks, warehouses, huge radar systems, satellite dishes, broadcasting towers, and an impressive fleet of jeeps. The contrast with the poverty-stricken, precarious Palestinian controls could not be more glaring.

Along the entire southern perimeter, the roads opened up by the occupier link the settlements and are always lined by rolls of barbed wire and barriers, like a rich state within a poor state. Miserable flocks graze dunes and areas not cordoned off and some peasants grow olive trees and hedges of prickly pear on their plots. The traffic signs are exclusively in the language of the occupation: the agricultural farms of Gan Or Bdolach, Benel Atzmon. The dwellings destined for the settlers spread out, well ordered, elegant, with their white facades and red roofs: I notice that most are empty. Tsahal jeeps drive round unimpeded from one place to another: there is no barrier or checkpoint belonging to Arafat's police in the area. At the entrance to one abandoned secondary road, a sign warns in English: "Attention! You are entering the territory of the Palestinian National Authority!" By now inured to such surprises, I decide to take a look at the border post separating the strip from El Arich. There, between the decorative controls of the PNA and Arab Republic of Egypt, Israelis inspect and decide who leaves, who enters: no inhabitant of Gaza or foreign visitor can depart or set foot in the self-governing territory without their permission or stamp. The Pakistani ambassador in Cairo came there to prepare Benazir Bhutto's frustrated visit to Arafat, and had to retrace his steps with his tail between his legs. According to the most reliable statistics Tsahal still controls 42 percent of the Strip occupied by only thirty-seven hundred settlers. Some of the nineteen settlements, like the one in Netzarim, are uninhabited and apparently act as bases and sanctuaries for the armed or destabilizing actions of the *mustaarabin*, the Israeli agents who, disguised as Arabs, carry out *cleanup* operations against the "enemies of the peace process." Despite the Oslo Accords, and at the risk of increasing the hatred engendered by the occupation and the intolerable economic inequality, a military order of May 1994 authorized the confiscation of new lands for settlement northeast of Beit Lahia, in the far north of the autonomous territory.

Considering all the circumstances, it is not at all surprising that the greater the praise and homages to Arafat in the press and government circles of the United States and the European Union—the pompous ceremony in the White House, the presentation of the Nobel Prize shared with Rabin and Peres—the more his stature and credibility declines among the inhabitants of Gaza. Welcomed as a hero on reaching the Strip on 1 July 1994, his political line and method of governing are questioned by a growing sector of the population.

In his defense it must be said that responsibility for such disaffection is only partially his. After twenty-seven years of occupation and six of *intifada*, expectations of immediate, palpable changes were clearly unrealistic. But the PLO leader's projects, the conversion of Gaza into a Mediterranean Hong Kong or Singapore, aired in various interviews, were likewise rather ingenuous. "We will revolutionise living conditions," he promised soon after his arrival. "We will build 30,000 homes, and that means jobs for 50,000 workers. There'll no longer be any need to go to Erez in search of work in Israel."

Of the $720 million promised to the Palestinian National Authority in 1994, only $60 million have been received. Last September, at a meeting of donor countries, the issue of a small portion of funds destined for East Jerusalem prevented, as the result of pressure from Israel and the World Bank, the planned release of $200 million. Help from different countries (France, Japan, Norway, and so forth) is devoted to specific projects and the drip-feed grants authorized by Israel do not cover the running costs of the PNA agreed in Oslo and Cairo. In a word: Arafat lacks the means to carry through his policies, a victim both of Rabin's rug-pulling tactics and of an environment increasingly hostile to his "mini-protectorate" in Gaza.

In an interview given months ago to the Israeli daily *Haaretz*, the leader of the PNA expressed his despair at Israel's double dealiing, at the attempts to sabotage "the peace process" by extremists from both camps and the "daily humiliations" inflicted by his former enemy.

The restrictions imposed on the freedom of movement of

his "ministers" (sometimes prevented from going to Jericho or entering the West Bank); the refusal to allow him access to the holy Muslim places of Jerusalem (whereas King Hussein of Jordan was warmly invited to pray there); the successive deferrals of the calendar for Palestinian elections put off from 13 April to 15 December and delayed even further ("no date is sacred," was Rabin's laconic comment); the closure of the border to thousands of workers in an act of collective retaliation against the events in Erez (with a consequent worsening of social and political tensions in the Strip); the reiterated demand that the National Council of Palestine meet in Gaza to abrogate the articles of the National Charter that call for the total liberation of Palestine (a demand that was impossible to satisfy through lack of a quorum); the pressure on the PNA to arrest and sentence Hamas and Islamic Jihad militants whenever one of their members commits an attack in Israel or in the territories under its control (forcing him to take on the unhappy role previously played by Tsahal and thus condemning him in the eyes of his compatriots); the sharp decrease in the number of work permits in Israel for workers from the Strip, from eighty thousand to eight thousand (causing a loss of vital income for hundreds of thousands of people) and the decision to recruit labor in Romania, Thailand, and China (thirty-five thousand workers from these countries have already taken the place of Palestinians in the labor market), all these factors and elements demonstrate the real impotence of the veteran PLO leader caught in his lobster pot.

To this long list of obstacles and trials, one would have to add Rabin's wish to undermine symbolically the figure of his old, hounded rival: Arafat's two personal helicopters remain grounded in an Egyptian airport; the title he wanted of president of the PNA was downgraded to chairman and Hamas militants call him contemptuously *mendub* (delegate of Tel Aviv, one assumes); the right to print stamps with the name of Palestine was vetoed in Cairo . . .

If the general suffering of the population after years of martial law or curfew locked in the squalid slums of the camps has diminished, the concrete benefits of peace are nowhere to be seen. The reduction in jobs, shortfalls in the educational system, lack of infrastructure and medical care make for a somber panorama threatening the stability of the area and their leader's precarious situation. Although statistics show that Arafat still has more support than Hamas or the lay opposition of the Democratic Front for the Liberation of Palestine (DFLP) exiled in Damascus, I have found hardly anyone prepared to defend him openly.

From Haidar Adel Shafi—the respected president of the Islamic Red Cross, previously negotiator of the first peace conversations and intermediary between the PNA and Islamists after the recent massacre by the mosque in Gaza—to the university teachers, traders, and youths I have been able to talk to, the criticism of the Oslo Accords and Arafat's authoritarianism, arbitrariness, and clannish conception of power, whether ferocious or cautious, sybilline or bitter, leaves no room to doubt the gradual decline in his popularity.

"The peace process is losing all credibility," says Haidar Adel Shafi, "Rabin maintains total control of the situation: he wants to cantonalize the Palestinian territories and corner us in a series of *Bantustans*. Our people has the right to resist an occupation that has changed its name, but not its methods."

A bazaar owner in Omar al Mokhtar street argues vehemently that the situation has got worse with self-government and illustrates his point of view with a parable: "If a poor man is starving and a rich man gives him a fish, he will eat it gradually and be satisfied. If he doesn't give him anything, he will learn how to fish." An Arab tale or a maxim extracted from Mao's *Little Red Book?* The notes jotted down in my notebook included a dozen such commentaries. All in all, exhausted by six years of *intifada*, the majority of the population wants a respite and not renewed lethal confrontations. If the anticipated international help was invested in Gaza, the present tendency to inveigh against Arafat and dismiss him as a political corpse would probably be reversed. Meanwhile, the social situation is deteriorating and, according to estimates by Terje Larsen, the UN special coordinator for the occupied territories, "The population's standard of living has dropped 5o percent in the last six months."

One of the first measures adopted by the shiny new PNA was to clean anti-Israeli slogans off the walls of Gaza. The operation, which cost more than $3 million, according to the *New York Times*, proved to be as wasteful as it was futile. Weeks after the whitewashing the city looked just the same: slogans reappeared but now aimed against the head of the PNA: "Arafat, slave to Rabin and the Americans, your fate will be Sadat's!" After the bloody clashes belween police and Hamas rioters on 18 November 1994, the war of slogans and insults intensified. "Assassins of your own people, hell awaits you!" met counterthreats from Al Fatah Falcons: "We'll cut off the tongues of those who've sold out to Tehran!" Not all the slogans in Gaza are in the same mode. Some reveal an interest in the world situation: "Palestine, Iraq, Bosnia, Chechnya, aggression against Islam continues." Another, in the stadium where Hamas held a mass meeting on 16 December, is particularly sinister: "We'll pave the road to Paradise with skulls of Jews." In the outer districts of Gaza, the PLO leader's photograph often appears torn or paint-spattered. As an unemployed university teacher told me, a reader of von Clausewitz—"the peace process is occupation by other means"; "The Israelis are rubbing their hands together. Now we Palestinians are killing each other."

The Islamist movement in Gaza, heir to the Muslim brotherhood, rooted in the Strip for decades, initially renounced the political struggle against Israeli occupation in favor of religious and social proselytizing that posed no problems for the authorities in the Jewish state. Although PLO "cadres" were decimated by Sharoh's implacable repression between 1967 and 1971, Sheikh Ahmad Yasin's League for the Islamic Charter spread its activities through schools, clinics (for the poor), literacy campaigns, and help centers for refugees most in need. Like Boumedien and Chadli in Algeria in the 1970s and at the beginning of the 1980s, the occupiers looked warmly upon the mainly religious network of associations that acted as a useful counterbalance to the revolutionary and Marxist *fedayeen* of Yaser Arafat (Al Fatah), Georges Habache (PFLP), and Nayef Hawatmeh (DFLP). In fact—like the two Algerian presidents with the radical Islamism that would give rise to the FIS—they were playing with fire. The creation of Hamas in December 1987 didn't alarm the occupier, despite Sheik Yasin's condemnation of the PLO's acceptance of the UN Security Council resolution that proposed the creation of two states within the territory of the former British mandate of Palestine. With the spontaneous explosion of the *intifada* and the participation of Hamas, the Israeli attitude changed: Sheikh Yasin was arrested in May 1989 and was released after ten years in jail. But the prioritizing of the struggle against the PLO, judged to be the main enemy by Tel Aviv, allowed the Islamist organization to preserve its cadres and capacity for struggle from the roundups by Tsahal and Shin Beth (the secret services) until the beginning of the present decade. Although Arafat's peace initiatives were rejected by Tel Aviv and his leadership suffered the disastrous consequences of his suicidal political support for Saddam Hussein during the Gulf War, Hamas skillfully maintained its links with the moderate Arab states in the anti-Iraqi coalition, from which it received and probably still receives financial support.

From 1991, every development seemed to swing against the PLO leader: the breaking off of relations with the Saudis and Gulf emirates and loss of considerable economic aid; the end to the dispatch of money by Palestinian workers in the Middle East, life blood to tens of thousands of families in the occupied territories; international isolation; the difficulties and stumbling blocks in the peace process begun in Madrid; growing Islamist agitation against his policy "of capitulation." The confrontation between Palestinians did not overly worry the Israelis who, with surprising myopia or Machiavellian cunning, pretended not to notice that Arafat was no longer the Third World revolutionary of the good old days—his inner weakness and pariah status had transformed him into a valid, even docile interlocutor, ready to compromise with whatever was necessary for him to gain acceptance in Washington—whereas

Hamas—like the PLO at its inception—excluded any agreement with the "Zionist entity" until Palestine was totally liberated. When Tsahal and the Israeli security services opened their eyes, they suffered a major shock. "Hamas is like a hydra," one of Rabin's advisers on matters of antiterrorist struggle commented to a *Le Monde* journalist. "When we cut off its heads, others immediately grow in their stead."

BETWEEM HAMAS AND RABIN

The arrival of the PLO in Gaza deepened the conflict between the Palestinian National Authority and Hamas. Arafat countered the graffiti war and campaign to discredit him with interrogations, arrests, and roundups of Islamists. Comprising mainly soldiers from the Liberation Army who followed Arafat from Jordan to the Lebanon and from Lebanon to Tunisia before scattering to various "fraternal" countries, from Algeria to Yemen—the new Palestinian police acts in a disorganized, improvized way, with frequent recourse, according to accounts from impartial observers, to methods copied from the *mukhabarat* of various Arab dictatorships. Even more disturbing; the compartmentalization and rivalries dominating the different services generate a general atmosphere of uncertainty. By the side of the EU-financed national security and presidential guard there exist a blue-uniformed civilian police, a "deterrent" style political police based in Jericho under the command of the unpredictable, impetuous Jibril Rajub, a general information service, and a military information section. Such a proliferation of services and their expeditious, sometimes bitter internal struggles, particularly on the West Bank, rightly alarm numerous Palestinians, whether of democratic persuasion or Islamist leanings.

The suicidal acts that led to the death of three Israeli soldiers at the crossroads of the main road to Rafah and the settlement of Netzarim, the work of the Islamic Jihad and consequent roundup of 150 militants of that organization by the PNA police, brought thousands of Gaza youngsters to the streets led by the two Islamist organizations, in a protest rally demanding their immediate release: the demonstrators chorused anti-Israeli slogans and denounced "Arafat's collusion with Rabin." In controversial circumstances—versions of what happened are diametrically opposed—the police, which on Friday, 18 November, came to the mosque to confiscate the loudspeakers of the orators, was pelted with stones and responded with bullets: several people were killed. The confrontations spread to the whole strip over the next twelve hours, accompanied by pillaging, physical attacks, and fires. Angry and distressed, Gaza relived the worst moments of the *intifada*. The balance sheet of the repression: thirteen dead. The PNA provided another version of the facts and spoke of "outside provocation": some detected the hidden hand of Israel and its *mustaarabin*. According to various accounts, several policemen threw their weapons to the ground and refused to obey orders from their superiors. Others followed orders like policeman Ayman Badhi who, devoured by remorse, deserted the barracks where he was serving, wrote a farewell letter to his family, and carried out a frustrated suicide attack on a Jerusalem bus. A photo of him, Kalashnikov in hand, is on display in numerous bazaars and public places in Gaza.

Very significantly, during the turmoil of Black Friday Hamas militants set fire to the only two cinemas in the enclave, which had been reopened after their enforced closure during the *intifada: nasir* (the Victory), in the crowded avenue of Omar al Mokhtar in Gaza and *Shahid* (the Martyr) in Rafah.

"Islamists oppose all cultural and artistic activities which communicate decadent Western ideology," a mustachioed, bespectacled youth quips ironically while photographing the *naser*'s devastated facade. "It's quite ridiculous, don't you think? From this perspective, we should pull up all the grapevines on the pretext that they produce wine. But don't they also provide all the grapes we eat?"

It seems difficult to bridge the gap between Hamas and the PNA. The Islamists vehemently accuse Arafat of having sold out on the "sacred goals" of the Resistance: the return to their homes of all refugees from 1948, the reconquest of the whole of the occupied territory, and the founding of a Palestinian state with its capital in Jerusalem. According to Yusef Ibrahim, the *New York Times* correspondent, those arrested from the movements opposed to the so-called "peace process" employ the pitiless tactic of answering their interrogators in Hebrew (many Gaza youths learned the language during their stay in jail) and address them using the humiliating term *Katzin* (an Israeli army officer). Are we on course to the much feared Palestinian civil war that some predict and many desire?

After a zigzag drive through mudflats and water-logged streets, Sami drives me to my rendezvous with Mahmud Zahar, one of Hamas's most respected leaders, whose home was recently machine-gunned by an unidentified group. His critique of the Oslo Accords and Washington declaration of principles is biting and harsh.

"How can anyone talk of peace if we are still at war, with 95 percent of our territory still under Israeli control? Arafat has surrendered and exacted nothing in exchange. His economic plans have collapsed and he's forced to go begging to Rabin and Clinton. Why does he allow six thousand Palestinians, many from his own political group, to rot in Israeli prisons? Why does he require so many police if not to repress his own people? Who elected him to the office he enjoys? We want open, honest elections."

Although we talked of more general issues — Bosnia, Algeria, Chechnya — my interlocutor, despite his criticisms of the GIA's terrorism, defends the right of the Algerian Islamists to execute soldiers and other agents of the Junta like *singers*. "Singers?" I repeated, thinking I had misheard him. "Yes, singers in the pay of a corrupt, atheist state."

When I said good-bye, despite making every effort, I wasn't able to return his friendly smile.

Nighttime in Gaza is a sad affair: no street lights, very few cafés, and restaurants that close early, as if subject to an imaginary curfew, the few night owls who venture down the potholed streets and submit to police control barriers usually rendezvous in one of the two hotels on the seafront: businessmen, civil servants, the odd foreigner, journalist, or member of the UNPRP or another humanitarian association. The only Gaza women with uncovered heads I saw were there or at the PNA headquarters.

From my bedroom window, at daybreak—there are no

blinds or curtains and I wake up with the dawn—I gaze down on the ghostly skeleton of the dock. Arafat's ambitious project to open up the Strip to international trade with a port able in a first phase to accommodate boats of over five thousand tons—an enterprise theoretically subsidized by European aid that never arrived—collapsed last November when a storm blasted to smithereens the quay that was under construction. The rocks brought from Jericho to protect metal stanchions from the onslaught of the waves had been seized months earlier by the Israelis at the Erez frontier post on the pretext that the building work in the port did not have the support of the Israeli-Palestinian joint commission that finances economic projects in the area. For the same reason, the garbage trucks donated by France to the Gaza Town Hall, school materials sent by humanitarian associations, and computers and spare parts from various nongovernmental organizatons are held back by Israeli customs in the port of Ashdod and at the Egyptian frontier. According to *Le Monde* of 21 January 1995, some of these gifts seem to "have gone astray" or to have been sold at public auction without the least public protest from the countries or organizations affected by such an arbitrary use of power: in Oslo everything was "well and truly sorted!"

Arafat was not discouraged by Israeli obstructionism and carried on with his project but the "expert" advising him proved to be a charlatan. Today, the battered, rickety pontoon hangs there like a centipede in the sea, twisted, pathetic, and mangled.

There is little movement in the neighboring fishing port, which is out of bounds to the public. Fishermen can only work within an area of twenty kilometers along the Strip, beyond which their boats are relentlessly hauled in by Israeli patrols. That makes fish a luxury item, beyond the means of the majority of pockets.

Three hundred meters from the hotel, between the coast and a spacious car park, stands the modest, squat building of the Palestine National Authority. National Security Police and the presidential guard chat peacefully at the entrance, check out visitors, and effusively greet public figures coming to do business with "ministers." Among those waiting to be let in on the opposite side, I notice a man in his seventies, a wizened face and greying mustache, dressed in a grey djellaba and wearing a spotlessly white *kaffiyeh:* I am struck by his noble, austere bearing and regret I haven't brought my Pentax in order to take his photograph. Although a friend has given me Yasir Abed Rabbo's direct number, the "minister" of culture and information—one of the most courageous, independent members of the PNA—I prefer to follow the normal routines and experience the ways of the new administration. I show my passport and letter of accreditation and, to my surprise, am let through. I settle down in a room surrounded by half a dozen offices and observe the toing and froing of employees, secretaries, and police. After a while, a functionary informs me that the minister will see me at two P.M. I give him a copy of my letter of accreditation and he tells the police on duty at the door to let me in on my return without further formalities. I appear at two o'clock but the guard has changed, the minister is attending a cabinet meeting and, when I ask for my letter back, nobody knows its whereabouts: it's been mislaid.

Someone advises me to come back in an hour's time: the meeting must end at three o'clock and there will be a press conference. Amused and intrigued, I sit down on the edge of the opposite sidewalk. The noble-looking old man is still pacing up and down, staring at the inaccessible building. A group of women want to talk with Arafat: they are widowed or divorced and complain of being harrassed by police prowling round their houses at night and ringing their doorbells. A jovial, stout policeman keeps them at a friendly distance. Journalists and cameramen from the local weekly *Philistine* and the modest autonomous television channel, visible only in part of the Strip—the satellite disks of a booster station donated by France rust at the border, awaiting finicky Israeli permissions—gather for the end of the "council of ministers" with a touching faith in the transcendence of that event and rush in with their cameras, microphones and booms to interview Nabil Shaath. He cuts the interview short and disappears in one of the official PNA cars. Another "minister" is in turn waylaid by the representatives of the means of communication. Neither the women nor the old man in the djellaba and *kaffiyeh* manage to get near him. Other vehicles drive off. A friend informs me that Yasir Abed Rabbo has just left for Jericho. From my observation post on the curb, the scene strikes me as rather Felliniesque.

It is my last afternoon in Gaza and I decide to take advantage of the voracious seasonal light to contemplate some beauty spot (or have yesterday's occupiers and today's sentinels also suppressed every scrap of beauty on the Strip?). Outside the urban sprawl, a road runs southward along the coast. We stop with Sami at a beach where the bars are closed and where two youths are resting in a cart pulled by a donkey. Several houses with sea views are evidence of the timid emergence of a bourgeoisie (the projected building program of private housing has not prospered as foreseen because of a lack of finance, Israeli bureaucratic holdups, and internal quarrels between the company backed by donor countries and Arafat's administration. After a brief stroll, we drive on along a half-abandoned road, near the Israeli settlement of Netzarim, till we meet up with a bus full of schoolkids taken out by their teachers to run and play on the beach. It is a proud and austere landscape and after a few blasts of fresh sea air, we turn back.

Unexpectedly, a vehicle bristling with police blocks our way. The police point their machine guns at us and force me to step out onto the side of the road. They scrutinize the taxi from hood to trunk while I hand over my passport to the person who seems to be the officer in charge. After the car search Sami is "invited" to get into the truck, three youths pile into the taxi with me, and we set off at top speed to an unknown destination. The one driving at my side turns on the radio and puts the volume on maximum. The three police—in their early twenties—seem excited, and euphoric, and I soon find out why. In spite of the deafening noise from the radio I catch one or two snatches of conversation. They

think they have caught a big fish: an Israeli colonel or commander! "Yu'r not Spanis," the driver rasps angrily. I find my
captors' glee endearing and resolve to keep quiet: it seems
cruel to deprive them of a few minutes' pleasurable revenge.
The vehicle bursts into the city Hollywood-style and my
chauffeur hoots his horn triumphantly at the entrance to the
security headquarters. There, I am led into a small office as
another set of guards deal with Sami. The questioning begins
curtly, then gradually softens. My numerous visas and passport stamps from Arab and Muslim states are intriguing (they
also intrigued the police at Tel Aviv airport to the point that,
although I asked her not to stamp my passport so as not to
invalidate my Lebanese visa, the passport controller did so
without batting an eyebrow). I am careful to avoid using my
North African dialect: that might perhaps complicate my situation because it is used by many Israelis of Moroccan origin.
After checking that I am resident in the hotel I named, the
officer returns my passport.

"Our apologies. There are Israeli infiltrators in this area. A
few days ago we arrested ten in an orange grove near Kir
Beit El Adat. Didn't you read about it in the press?" He tries
to offer me tea but I invent an appointment elsewhere as an
excuse.

"Your green trousers and backpack confused my men.
They thought you were a soldier."

As I say good-bye, we shake hands and I promise that in
the future I'll wear a different outfit.

One would need a whole book to do justice to Gaza: its
poverty, oppression, brazenness, feeling of neglect, suffoca-
tion, a violent backlash after so many faded illusions, so
many dreams come to nought.

"Look at the youth in the camps," a teacher told me. "They
live crammed in together, no work, no distractions, no possibility of migrating abroad or starting a family. A large percentage of them were tortured or arrested during the *intifada*.
They all have at least some brothers, relatives, or friends who
are martyrs and they've stayed in their ghettoes like animals

for weeks on end. Gradually they feel it's a living death and their hearts turn into bombs. Then one day, without informing the family, they run off with whatever weapon they can grab on a suicide terrorist mission. They're not worried about dying because they feel they're already dead."

I'll leave in the inkpot, for the moment, the story of Alia, the woman who owns Marna House, where I lodged at the beginning of my stay and whose biography someone should write one day as a compendium of a pitiless History of the Children of the City. Without noticing, I've also caught the lucid pessimism of its inhabitants and their anguished feeling of being suffocated.

The next day I pack my suitcase and return with Sami to the Erez border crossing. The taxi with an Israeli license plate is already waiting for me and this time I queue up with workers from the Strip at the control posts where they check my passport and let me depart the obsessive, infamous ghetto that is Gaza, with mixed feelings of impotence and sorrow.

THE DIVIDENDS OF PEACE?

In Jerusalem I head for my old haunt, the American Colony Hotel. As it was six years ago, the ground-floor bar and lounges—the patio is unfortunately closed because of the seasonal cold—are the obligatory meeting points for journalists, Palestinian intellectuals, politically conscious or cultured tourists and, this is a novel development, Jordanian executives and businessmen—most being Palestinians resident in Jordan—and now in East Jerusalem to study the prospects for investment opened up by the "peace process."

Strategically situated halfway between the European Consulate district and the road leading to the walled precinct of the Old City, the American Colony is barely one hundred meters from Orient House, the Palestinian cultural institution that embodies the spirit of resistance of those inhabitants of Jerusalem to the Israeli authority's policy of compulsory annexation. From there I can walk along Salah El Din Street after passing by St. George's Cathedral and the Albright Institute and peer into shops, stores, bookshops, kiosks, and *bureaux de change*. When I come out onto the avenue that goes round the old walls, I only have to swing to the right, amid the bustle of street traders and the chaos of the bus station, to cross the road and walk down the steps leading to the crowded Damascus Gate.

During the *intifada*, the streets within the walls were almost always deserted, patrolled by Tsahal soldiers with their threatening Uzis and M-16s. Tourists were few and far between and orthodox Jews from the synagogues installed in the heart of the Christian-Palestinian area also carried weapons and strode up and down the streets. The spectacle from the gate in January 1995 is much more attractive and enticing. Café terraces are full, street sellers hawk their wares on the stepped slope, and solitary tourists or groups photograph the scene, sniff round the bazaar displays, and haggle over prices. For a few seconds I feel at home: the familiar atmosphere of Djemaa el-Fna.*

---

*The great public square in the city of Marrakesh.

I take El Oued Street and constantly bump into Orthodox priests, Armenian monks, Franciscan friars, Sisters of Charity, rabbis, and students from some Koranic school. The fertile plurality of cultures seems once more to be flourishing at the point where the three great monotheist religions converge. I can make out a bazaar with a Spanish name: Ciudad Santa Recuerdos, at the entrance to which flaps the pendant of a mysterious "Colombian Battalion" (its owner is probably a Palestinian who got rich in that country). Tsahal soldiers still guard the building occupied by Ariel Sharon, topped by a large Jewish candelabra and decorated with an Israeli flag that hangs down over the facade. Nobody now deigns to take any notice of it (before, it was regularly pelted with stones) and foreign visitors mingle with the faithful going to daily prayers in the mosque of al-Aksa, on the esplanade of the Dome.

The impression of normality is an illusion, I was told hours later by a professor of Birzeit university, a friend of the great Palestinian poet Mahmud Darwish. The mayor of Jerusalem, Ehud Olmert, a leading member of the hawkish wing of the Likud Party, is trying every possible tactic to close down Orient House—the general headquarters of the PLO and its supporters—as well as the other Palestinian cultural institu-tions to transfer them to Gaza and Jericho: its employees are subject to administrative pressure and holdups (confiscation of documents and passes, summonses to military security head-quarters, interrogations, and so on). The Israelis have com-pleted and strengthened their seige of the Old City through the construction of new districts linked by motorways that isolate and stifle the already scarce "strongholds" of the enemy; Arabs living in Jerusalem require special permits to build, repair, and extend their dwellings; all the plots they could have claimed in a radius of twenty kilometers have been expropriated by decree. As the Dutch geographer Jan de Jong writes—quoted by Edward Said—the new Israeli colonies encircle the capital in swathes, the last of which will stretch from Birzeit in the north to the suburbs of Hebron in the south, the Greater Jerusalem under construction will thus encompass almost 25 percent of the occupied territory of the West Bank.

In a taxi with a Palestinian driver but an Israeli license plate, I begin my journey to the area denominated Judea and Samariah by the settlers. The road leading to Ramallah which I traveled so often years ago with the Spanish television crew suffers the same snarl-ups as the busiest roads crossing the capital. Halfway there, Tsahal has established a powerful control mechanism: cars with blue West Bank license plates can't enter the Holy City if they don't have a special permit. Consequently, Palestinians authorized to cross the Green Line of the old 1948 borders to work in Israel prefer to leave their cars in a nearby parking lot: traders, old people, the sick with the necessary medical prescriptions, children enrolled in schools in East Jeruslaem, and so on, must wait in interminable queues to deal with frontier formalities before squeezing into the packed buses with Israeli plates that cover the journey to Jerusalem.

As denounced by Sister Paula Teresa, the secretary of the Commission for Justice and Peace, resident in Ramallah (*Le Monde Diplomatique*, March 1993), controls and hassles continue even inside the buses: "Yesterday, after being packed with great difficulty into one of them, we were stopped a hundred metres further on: a fresh check on our identity cards. You have to have seen the trapped look of a man at the mercy of a soldier threatening to tear up his precious, indispensible document before confiscating it, to understand how the accumulated hatred one feels at so much humiliation will one day explode in the face of those generating it. In such a situation, any spark may light the fire. After forcing everyone to get off the bus, six men had their documentation impounded, including the driver. We departed Ramallah at six A.M. and finally reached Jerusalem at nine o'clock: three hours to travel 15 kilometers."

On the other side of the "border" the panorama changes completely—the great paradox of the occupation arises from the fact that by extending the radius of its settlements to the whole of Palestine the settler is forced to perpetuate the borders recognized internationally from 1948 to 1967, to reduce the insecurity of Israel itself and the 140,000 settlers in the

144 Jewish centers on the West Bank—the *mukhayam* or Palestinian camp of Qalandiya, adjacent to the main roadway, has disappeared. Without its fence, streets walled off or blocked by empty oil drums, or watch posts, it is difficult to trace. The road to Ramallah bustles, animated by garages, mini-markets, furniture stores, real estate agents, and rental car firms. The numerous television aerials have strange silvery Eiffel Tower shapes. Tsahal controls are discreet and seem to vanish as we enter the city.

For years Ramallah lived in a climate of daily war: on indefinite general strike, businesses and shops were closed, and its painfully empty streets looked desolate and deathly. Israeli jeeps patrolled from one end to another and sentinels posted on roofs aimed submachine guns at the scant passersby: women, children, old people . . .

Today, bottlenecks hold up the traffic in the center and it is almost impossible to park. Street vendors invade the pavements, and bareheaded boys and girls eye windows replete with the articles of modern technology. The Arab Bank, Bank of Jordan and Cairo-Amman Bank have established new headquarters; capital from the Hashemite kingdom circulates and is invested under the occupier's benevolent gaze. Numerous Palestinians with Jordanian nationality have purchased or are building houses and firms, convinced that one day or another Ramallah will be the capital of the small Palestinian or Palestinian-Jordanian entity tolerated or backed by Israel.

Although Arafat was forced to give up his ambition to create a Palestinian Bank with the power to issue money and was obliged to temporarily allow the Israeli shekel into the enclaves of Gaza and Jericho, Jordanian dinars flood into the West Bank after the peace agreements signed by King Hussein and Rabin. The strategy of Jordanian penetration of its old dominions thus complements Israel's more ambitious plan: this Common Market of the Middle East of which Tel Aviv, with the wholehearted backing of the United States, will be the engine and guiding spirit. After Oslo and the Washington Declaration, nobody can accuse King Hussein of

breaking "Arab solidarity" or "betraying the sacred cause of
Palestine": Arafat set the precedent. In this way, with no trace
of a guilty conscience, the Hashemite kingdom is moving its
pawns on to the other bank of the Jordan while Rabin stran-
gles Gaza and leaves the PNA in an untenable position. In
contrast with the potential opened up by future political freedom associated with Jordan, the Gaza-Jericho option seems
daily less attractive or feasible. A survey carried out by the
Naphisa Institute of Palestinian Research (Nablus) reveals that
46 percent of the inhabitants of the occupied West Bank favor
union or a confederation with the Hashemite kingdom as
against 52 percent who defend a Palestinian state. In East
Jerusalem, the percentage of the former rises to 58 percent.
Despairing of a return to the borders of 1948 and subjected
to the difficulties, upsets, and hassles of daily life, ten thousand Palestinians, according to the *Jerusalem Post,* have
already requested Israeli nationality. The glee with which the
Likud mayor spread the news may, however, be short-lived:
the growing number of Israeli Arabs is a double-edged sword
and in the medium term will give Israel a set of insoluble
problems and new challenges.

In any case, Ramallah constitutes the best example of the
interlocking of Israeli-Palestinian-Jordanian projects and of
the Machiavellianism or blindness of Rabin's policies: a small
island of relative economic prosperity entirely surrounded by
shantytowns, the fruit of colonial hardheadedness completely
at odds with the objectives of the so-called "peace process."

The normalization of life in Ramallah fades once past the
Jalazun crossroads, where years ago we witnessed a spectacular incursion of schoolchildren throwing stones at Tsahal
vehicles. A few kilometers farther on, as we descend into the
valley, an Israeli control barrier blocks our way: the main
road to Nablus has been closed to traffic; we must take the
long mountain detour along a road passing near Birzeit. Once
again, we drive through Mediterranean landscapes with olive
groves, cultivated terraces, white sandy soil, drystone walls,
and prickly pears. Across the ridge of the surrounding mountains, with an obviously strategic intent, the ideological set-

tlements of occupiers mainly from the U.S. cordon off the landscape with their bunkers, barbed-wire fences, and watchtowers. Tsahal creates leveled space in the tormented configurations of the land, shatters the beauty and harmony, extends its net in a spider's web surrounding villages and hamlets. Just over a year after the Oslo Accords, Israel has confiscated more than seven hundred square kilometers of Palestinian land, uprooted more than fifteen thousand fruit trees to establish its settlements, and controls 73 percent of the fifty-seven hundred square kilometers of the West Bank of Jordan occupied in 1967. Moreover, its administration has taken over 80 percent of the water resources for its own ends. Doesn't this constitute a violation of the Madrid agreements in virtue of which Washington granted credits of $10 million to Israel on condition that it "froze" its colonization of Gaza and the West Bank? That issue does not seem to particularly worry those who make decisions on the ground. They are the winners and are not wracked by scruples in relation to the defeated.

After our roundabout trip through the mountains we return by the main road to Nablus. The reason for the diversion, as I later discover, is a demonstration by settlers trying to establish themselves in the spot where the Israeli Ofra Felix was murdered on Friday, 6 January. "Wherever Jewish blood is spilt we will create a settlement," goes the placard. Although the military administration will not authorize the initiative—the place is very vulnerable to eventual attacks—several tents maintain a permanent guard about one hundred meters from the barrier closing the control road.

In June 1988, Tsahal cordoned off the village of Beit Furik for two weeks, for the perceived crimes of refusing to pay taxes being demanded and of being the home of the terrorist who murdered the mayor of Nablus, accused of collaborating with the occupiers. On the night of 17 June, it finally attacked the village with jeeps, trucks, and a helicopter. The operation ended with a large number of wounded and the death of the youth Husein Ahmed Mleitat, who was apparently hit by a bullet in the back. With the Spanish television

team we filmed the grave with his photo and Palestinian flags
at the foot of the mosque before giving our condolences to
the family, in a comfortable house at the top of the village. I
tell the driver to take the road into the village; it is abandoned
and full of potholes like all roads in the Palestinian areas cut
off from the ultramodern network linking the occupied lands
and the satellites created around them. Past refuse dumps—
the Israelis unload their rubbish on the future land of
autonomous Palestine—we cross extensive tracts of cultivated land and groves of fruit trees before entering the village, the memory of which remains pristine in my mind,
despite the years gone by. But at the spot in the square
where we filmed the protest demonstration there are now
two new buildings, the mosque is being repaired, and small,
open shops and parked vehicles show life has returned to a
more normal course, that the people can breathe. I look for
the boy's family: a young kid tells me his father is in the fields
and runs to tell him. I wait by the spot where the son fell and
minutes later Husein Ahmed Auda arrives, dressed in a grey
jacket and smock and wearing the traditional black-and-white
kaffiyeh. His eager eye recognizes me and we embrace
warmly. Life goes on, he says. Six more youths died in the
village; but now the situation is quiet, people go about their
business, and Tsahal leaves them in peace. He offers me and
the taxi driver a cup of tea and wants to invite us to lunch. I
tell him I must drive on to Nablus, promise to send him a
video of the film, and we say good-bye wishing each other
good luck.

The main road soon takes us into the center of the city. Like
Ramallah, its streets are bustling, lively, and congested with
traffic. Once again, the impression of normality overlays hidden tensions. The nooks and crannies in the bazaar remind me
of Fez or Marrakesh: the confusion of private and public space,
the concentration of things and people. Each face seems to
have its history etched on it: years of harsh living conditions.
  Suddenly, as we are returning to the square where we
parked, the mirage evaporates. We hear shouts and the

whines of police sirens. A youth has thrown a stone at an Israeli soldier and a group of soldiers rushes at a youth not involved in the incident, throws him to the ground, kicks him hard, and drags him to the jeep, where he remains hand-cuffed and facedown while they wait for reinforcements. People contemplate the scene from a safe distance and only one small bald man approaches the soldiers, tries to argue with them, and is pushed aside. A minute later there are half a dozen jeeps: their occupants flourish submachine guns and force onlookers to move back. When they finally drive off with their booty, I walk over to talk to the bald gentleman: someone explains to me in English that he is the boy's father. I can bear witness to his innocence and do so in writing, adding my signature and details. The family—in the mean-time, the arrested boy's mother and sister have arrived—beg me to go and give a statement at the local barracks. With my improvized English interpreter—I have learned from experi-ence not to admit to my Arabic—we go to the reinforced door, argue with the guard, and after a wait, are allowed down a corridor with metal detectors to the patio where the police has its quarters. There I reel off the reason for my visit and a dark-skinned youth, obviously a Jew originating from an Arab country, harangues me in Hebrew. His forehead is lightly bleeding: he was the one hit by the stone. I want to answer him in English but my companion dissuades me: "he says if you don't speak Hebrew your statement is worth noth-ing." His face is seething with hatred and suddenly I see a connection with the features of the driver of the group of Palestinian police who "captured" me in Gaza: you could eas-ily take them for twin brothers! How can there be such an abyss of incomprehension and loathing between almost iden-tical youths. The symmetry of the two situations fascinates me: nothing better sums up the intimate, visceral rage of this confrontation between brothers.

To spend time in the occupied territories of Palestine is to enter a universe of signs: that destabilizing mixture of "nor-mality and strangeness, of involvement and distance" that

Camille Mansour talks about in a short essay in *La revue d'études palestiniennes*. Dress, accent, and car license plates are signs forcing those who live in the border zone to identify or disassociate with one camp or the other. If the yellow tag endows the car with an Israeli identity, my Palestinian driver is very careful to display prominently the Arabic advertisement for the East Jerusalem taxi firm when he is crossing through Palestinian towns and villages, though he doesn't risk being stoned as he once might have. For the same reason, he removes the card when approaching an Israeli control post. My Moroccan accent may make me appear a Jewish emigrant from that country and I am careful not to use it with Palestinians I don't know in order not to arouse their suspicions. The same dialect, used with friends, however, will facilitate entry to a common emotional area and abolish distances. A foreigner in sunglasses and carrying a camera will be stopped from entering the precinct of Haram El Sharif at prayer time; without glasses and camera, holding a very visible copy of the daily *al-Quds* and an Islamic rosary, he will walk in unchallenged.

My apprenticeship in such semiology is in the end disturbing. What is the status of a frontier being? Person or sign?

SEPARATED AND ENMESHED

The journey south, toward Hebron, provides anyone observing the Palestinian drama with new situations close to familiar contexts that bring disquiet.

We take the side road through the olive groves of Gethsemane and reach the intersection with the main road which, beyond Hebron, cuts like a knife through the Neguev Desert. The old, often romantic villas of the Palestinian bourgeoisie in East Jerusalem have been occupied by Israeli families and the district is ethnically homogeneous, in keeping with the Likud Party's annexationist plans, carefully enacted by Mayor Ehud Olmert. A few kilometers on, the Greater Jerusalem border checkpoint filters cars with Jordanian license plates and Palestinians who are on their way to work or who have permission to visit the Holy City. Our car slips easily between the silent, resigned queues and the parked vehicles with blue license plates. Nobody in Israel or in the occupied territories asks us for our documentation. We are blessed by the omnipresent language of signs. What would happen, I wonder, if my complexion were darker and I sported a beard?

Past a Bethlehem mainly inhabited by Palestinian Christians, I notice to my left an entire district surrounded by metal fences, with entrances blocked by empty oil drums, as in the days of the *intifada*. I stop to find out what is happening and easily find a way in by a side passage. There are no Israeli police or watchposts. The area, I am told, has been punished: some youngsters took advantage of the slope to stone patrols driving in the vicinity. Now to enter by car you must take a diversion round the hill where the district nestles. The youth who is my guide says that one night he was beaten up in his home by a commando who burst in and threatened his parents.

Once more we pass through Alicantine landscapes, with carefully stepped terraces, like geological strips or layers of a map painted in different shades of ochre. In El Kadir the shops are shut and several Tsahal jeeps mount guard at the crossroads. The settlers from the neighboring settlement of Efrat have occupied new land and uprooted the trees: on state television I have seen images of verbal confrontations and exchanges of insults under the vigilant gaze of soldiers who keep the adversaries apart.

The settlements established or under construction continue along the main road, small prefabricated, red-roofed houses, caravans providing temporary accommodation for emigrants from Russia and North America, watchtowers, metal gates, and barbed wire: Neveh Daniel, Elazar, Efrat, Rosh Tzurim, Alon Schvut, Kfar Etzion.

A careful survey of the landscape of the West Bank reveals an incredibly patchwork structure. Barbed-wire fences surround settlements and military posts as well as areas being punished. They protect and exclude, unite separated areas and separate adjacent areas, and weave a labyrinth of islands that mutually repel and attract each other. In some places it is difficult to distinguish what they include and what they exclude, the inside from the outside. A complex capillary system for the circulation of traffic is evidence of the occupiers' desire to fragment the territory into plots, strips, and allotments that seem to become enmeshed, although they ignore each other.

I write these lines as the press announces the bloody terrorist attack in Netanya, in which nineteen Israelis perished. The uproar caused by the butchery further radicalizes the confrontation between the two peoples. When Yitzhak Rabin states that, to end these suicide attacks by human bombs, the "only solution lies in the total separation of Israel and the (occupied) territories" he is quite right. Palestinians and Israelis have to be separated if they ever aspire to live together in the future and share equally the land and natural resources of the former British mandate. But how can this separation be achieved if the policy of creating new colonies in Gaza and the West Bank spawns ever more clash points and makes it impossible? How can the security of Israelis be guaranteed in the tangled web of roadways that crosses hostile territory? Will there be a guardpost every one hundred meters? How to prevent them being shot at from a nearby hill?

Arafat's repeated apologies whenever there is a terrorist attack are logical and consistent with the so-called "peace process." But this concern for the safety of Israelis, so often detailed by Rabin and Peres in their meetings, should also be accompanied publicly with an equal concern for the lives, work, and dignity of Palestinians. These are never mentioned by Israeli negotiators who, from a position of strength, request guarantees that can only be effective on the basis of reciprocity. While Israel refuses to question its policy of occupation at any price and the "peace process" continues the occupation by other means, animosity and hatred in vast sectors of the two peoples will only intensify.

Entry into Hebron suddenly immerses me in the tense atmosphere of the years of the *intifada*. All shops, stores, and businesses are closed following a strike call against provocations by extremist settlers entrenched in the city center. Only chemists' shops and the fruit and vegetable market remain open. I drive around the other mountainous side of the city from whence one can survey the housing occupied and expropriated militarily by the intruders, recognizable at a distance from the presence of soldiers with submachine guns on roofs and terraces. In the immediate area of the Tombs of the Patriarchs, bazaars have been closed down and side streets blocked off with oil drums. After a brief conversation with my driver, the Israeli guards let the taxi through.

The great mosque sheltering the tombs of the Prophet venerated at once by Jews, Christians, and Muslims is an imposing building of ochre-colored stone. Its crenellations and domes remind me of some Spanish churches and cathedrals. The architectural hybridity also reflects the existence of centuries of cohabitation by the faithful of the three religions of the Book. It has a square minaret, with a kind of lookout destined for the muezzin and a small dome topped by three golden balls and a crescent.

Ever since the 25 February 1994 massacre, access to the tombs has depended on a complicated system of segregation: the mosque has been divided into two hermetically sealed parts. Devout Jews go in via the main staircase and must deposit their weapons before going through the metal detector controlled by Tsahal. I join a group of U.S. Ashkenazis and observe with them the tomb of the prophet Abraham or Ibrahim; the sepulchre is wrapped in a green cloth decorated with Islamic verses. Jewish visitors can peer inside through a wrought-iron padlocked door. Farther on, in the courtyard to the mosque, the Israelis have set up a small synagogue where students are reciting their prayers. In another room off the courtyard, several women seated on two rows of benches are chanting prayers opposite another wrought-iron door: Sarah's tomb. After taking a snapshot of the small fountain for ritual washing, whose green dome and crescent bear evidence of a fanatic's vandalism, I retrace my steps, go down the stairs, and turn the corner by the Tsahal control point to walk up the side reserved for Muslims. An Israeli soldier is guarding the entrance next to the metal detector and I mingle with the mosque faithful in the place where Baruch Goldstein, with the probable complicity of some Tsahal soldiers or officers, emptied the magazine of his submachine gun at the congregation, causing the deaths of twenty-nine people before he was lynched. Accompanied by a guide, I examine the *mihrab* and its marble columns, the cedar-wood pulpit or the *minbar,* its sides painted green and graceful white, black, and ochre striped stone pedestals. The prophet's tomb is visible through another iron door similar to the one on the shrine's Jewish side. The devotees of the nabi Ibrahim and his wife offer their prayers, ignoring the presence a few meters away of believers from the other community. Immediacy and exclusion, ours and theirs, symbolize here more than anywhere the stubborn anger of Israelis and Palestinians, the difficult, not to say impossible distribution of a common religious and cultural inheritance. As someone straddling the frontier, able to look on both sides, I reconstruct the mosque's original design and its present partition. How can one emerge unharmed from this daily schizophrenia?

The press and other Western news media follow very attentively, with justified alarm, the increase of Islamic fundamentalism from North Africa to Indonesia, but refer only in passing to other fundamentalisms that are no less disturbing or energetic: the Jewish, Hindu, Serbian, and Greek Orthodox varieties. The crime committed by Baruch Goldstein was not the work of someone "mentally unbalanced," as ran the verdict of the court that judged the massacre: it is the product of a radical Zionism rooted in the United States, infected in turn by the Messianism of the descendants of the Pilgrims with their ideal of Manifest Destiny and the climate of violence in the "ghettoised" societies of contemporary North American cities. In an enlightening essay on the subject ("A Third-Hand Moses," *El País*, 3 November 1991), Rafael Sánchez Ferlosio analyses the transfer, via America, of the colonizing mystique of the Protestant community—for whom the Indians were "at best a completely unnecessary people, and, at worse, inopportune, insistent phantoms that had to be put to flight, expelled and dispersed"—to the North American settlers installed on the West Bank. These extremist groups, like the one led by the infamous Rabbi Kahane, impose their law on numerous settlements, possessed by the idea that divine promise, the sense of history, and the present correlation of forces favor Israel: the existence of Palestinian ghettoes is neither surprising nor shocking since they grew up alongside the neighborhoods in conflict that envelop vast areas of Washington, Chicago, and New York. Their theocratic convictions are curiously symmetrical with those of the militants of Hamas and the Islamic Jihad. The photograph of the "hero" Baruch Goldstein is displayed in numerous settlements in the occupied territories as are ones of the shahid (martyr) Ayman Radhi in the refugee camps of Gaza. A lasting, just peace will never be possible except in opposition to the lethal combination of these two extremisms in conflict.

Since the attack in the mosque, Hebron has experienced an almost constant climate of confrontation. The ultraorthodox based in the center of the city have increased their provocations and continual clashes between the population and the army led to one dead and nineteen Palestinian wounded on 16 May. Two days later, two settlers were murdered and another seriously injured by Hamas militants. Despite the official presence of international observers, the situation worsens: violent demonstrations, curfews, general strikes, a return to situations experienced during the *intifada*. Although there were no serious incidents the day I visited— I only saw several youths being arrested and frisked—the tension is palpable. Tsahal paints over the anti-Israeli slogans on the metal shutters of stores and shops, but they reappear immediately. The idea of visiting Hebron's sights and monuments is not inviting. Better to return to Jerusalem.

On the journey there, a Tsahal control at the intersection with a secondary road leading to the Palestinian town of Beit Omar had convinced me that something foul was afoot there. On our return, the barrier has been removed but I decide to take a diversion and have a look. We search in vain for a café to have a cup of tea. Several bystanders in the square come and peer at the taxi, asking the driver who I am. A slim man in his thirties is hospitable and invites us into his home. We drive there with one of his younger friends, in jeans, a long green jacket, wearing a white-and-black *kaffiyeh* round his neck and sporting a trim beard. When I ask what has happened they reply that the night before, 8 January, Shin Beth (the Israeli secret police) arrived in the town and, for no reason, stopped the traffic of people and cars between the post office and the mosque. "I don't know whether they wanted a fight or to intimidate us," said the owner of the house. "What I do know is that they ordered the pavements to be cleared and two kids who were playing around were hit by rubber bullets. Eight-year-old Sari Hasan Awab was wounded in the leg and is in hospital in Hebron. Fawzi Faisal, a twenty-year-old, went to help him and was shot in the head. He has also been taken to hospital and we still don't know why these people came or why they attacked us so savagely. Yesterday I phoned a report to the newspaper *An Nahar* but they didn't publish it."

While we chat in the garden, the bearded youth in jeans explains to me that this type of so-called "deterrent" incursion often happens in spite of the peace accords. He and his friend were imprisoned during the *intifada* and they couldn't get permission to go to Jerusalem. Now they cultivate land and say they can't complain: others are having a much worse time.

The daily confrontations between the people of El Kadir and the settlers in Efrat continue. The Palestinians, supported by militants of the Israeli Peace Now movement, want to organize a protest march, but are dissuaded by a Tsahal officer. Several speakers, both Palestinian and Israeli, speak to a hundred demonstrators through megaphones. A few foreign radio and television teams record and film. I talk for a moment to the Antenne 3 correspondent and an Israeli girl coordinating the squats and actions in support of peasants threatened with expropriation. "Rabin is following the policies of Likud, humiliating and robbing Palestinians," she explains bitterly. "How can he talk of peace if the occupation continues and is being extended? It is a suicidal policy in the long term. With this kind of clash, why is anyone surprised if Palestinians take revenge and send their kamikazis into our cities?"

Two weeks later, the massacre in Netaya tragically proved the truth of her words.

DREAM AND NIGHTMARE

Can one talk of peace when since the solemn signing of the Washington Declaration on 13 September 1993 more than two hundred Palestinians have been killed by Tsahal or by settlers, over a hundred homes have been demolished by antitank weapons as a punishment, and fifteen thousand trees uprooted to make way for new settlements, not to mention the dozens of civilian and military Israeli victims of suicide attacks in Tel Aviv and Netanya?

This question posed by public opinion on both sides is answered in the affirmative by an ever-diminishing number of Israelis and Palestinians. The scenes of national mourning after the Netanya attack and the ill-concealed glee of the Gaza youths gathered outside the family homes of the human bombs show how the breach is widening between the two peoples—the colonizers and the colonized—rather than narrowing and healing. Thanks to the Israelis' blind arrogance and Arafat's vulnerabilty to pressure, we are witnessing the triumph of Cain: untrammeled hatred.

The restrained or openly hostile attitude of Palestinian intellectuals to the "peace process" has hardened as the latter swung from the path initiated in Madrid to slide down a slope of concessions unchallenged by Arafat leading ineluctably to the accords of Oslo and Cairo. The signing of the first round provoked an internal crisis in the leader's own organization: Faruk Kadumi, the PLO foreign affairs "minister" in Tunisia, boycotted the meeting of the PLO executive, as did Abu Mazen—who had nevertheless been one of the signatories. Gradually, several independent negotiators like Hanan Ashrawi, Haidar Adel Shafi, and others, abandoned ship, believing quite rightly that genuine peace requires a minimum of parity and evenhandedness. The poet Mahmud Darwish's resignation from the PNC (Palestinian National Council) and ex-member of the PNC, Edward Said's withering criticism of Arafat's "capitulation" and "autocratic methods" brought into the open the latter's growing lack of contact not only with the mass of marginalized youth in Gaza, won over to the cause of Hamas, but also, and even more seriously for him, from the Palestinian elite of the interior and the diaspora. Accusing him of throwing overboard Resolutions 242 and 338 of the UN Security Council on which the "peace process" was originally based, the signatories of a memorandum headed by Haidar Adel Shafi concluded that the swing by the Arafat leadership in Oslo and Cairo "validates illegal acts such as the Israeli establishment of colonies, the takeover of land, the annexing and Judaizing of Jerusalem, its isolation from the rest of the West Bank to give the final touches to Israeli hegemony in the occupied territories." Together with the secular opposition parties of the Rejection Front, most Palestinian intellectuals close until recently to the PLO believe that Arafat and his group have given up on the historic goals of the Resistance for very little reward: no return of all refugees to their homes or compensation for their losses; no return to the internationally recognised borders of the 1948 armistice; no creation of a sovereign state with its capital in East Jerusalem. We should add to that, as Edward Said reminds us, the abandoning "of the *intifada* and the very notion of resistance, not to mention the memory of all that has been destroyed or confiscated since 1948 whilst Israel has had to give up nothing substantial."

At the same time the Palestinians opened their eyes to the magnitude of the disaster—the third *nakba* or catastrophe in the last half century, according to a serene and dignified old lady in Gaza—the Israelis were chanting victory: the agreements signed in 1993 and 1994 are a new version, with slight variations, of the famous plan put forward by Deputy Prime Minister Ygal Alon just after the Israeli victory in the Six Day War. "They were the ones who changed their position, not us," declared Shimon Peres after the signing. "We are negotiating with a pale shadow of the old PLO." This initial glee was naturally in response to very tangible results: up to 1990, the United Nations defended a peaceful solution to the conflict based on the existence and mutual recognition of the two states. In Oslo and Cairo, the Palestinian state and the right to self-determination were shelved: Israel keeps control and holds sway over the Jordan valley, the borders of the PNA, the settlements and roads linking them, and greater Jerusalem, which the Knesset (the Israeli Parliament) unilaterally proclaims "the eternal, indivisible capital of the Jewish state." As Meron Benvenisti wrote in the Israeli daily *Ha'aretz* after the Cairo meeting in May 1994: "A careful reading of the hundreds of pages of the Accord leaves no doubt as to who won and who lost. Through all circumstantial wording, deliberate disinformation, hundreds of sections, sub-sections, appendices and protocols, it is crystal clear that the Israeli victory was crushing and the Palestinian defeat was absolute." To reward Rabin for his "flexibility" and "support for a just and equitable peace," the United States granted Israel aid worth more than $6 billion!

The question posed by a number of Palestinians as to how and why the ex-guerrilla leader backed agreements that "sold off at a bargain price"—in the words of Azmi Bichara, professor of philosophy, at the university of Birzeit—forty-five years of struggle is difficult to answer. The PLO's international isolation after the Gulf War and the sudden disappearance of its Soviet ally cannot explain everything. After more than twenty-five years of continuous wars, defeats, sieges, and exile during which it managed to defend and even spread support for its cause, were they forced by the growing gap between official revolutionary turns of phrase and the new realities created by the occupiers of their own country to look for an illusory "peace for the wicked"? Did the steamroller advances of the settlers that shrunk Palestinian territory like shark's skin cause them to conclude that, if they wanted to preserve the little that remained of their country, they had to get a move on before it disappeared entirely? The fact is that by sitting down at the negotiating table with no cards to play they were condemned to follow the game of the player holding all the trumps. The vagueness of the agreements legitimated an even more restrictive interpretation by the Israelis and opened the door to an (provisional?) autonomy without effective power, cut off from all aid and confronted by the inevitable discontent of the populace. By subscribing to the logic of its enemy—Israeli security both within the internationally recognized borders and in the occupied territories— with no reciprocity whatsoever, didn't the PLO realise that it was legitimating their conquests and its own dependency under conditions that were necessarily humiliating? It is very likely: Arafat faced the painful dilemma of negotiating a bad agreement or prolonging indefinitely the suffering of the population. It has to be recognized that in general terms this suffering has diminished relatively with the "peace process," but in the atmosphere of frustration now predominating nobody seems to take this fact into consideration.

As moderate Palestinian intellectuals point out, after decades of gradually confusing the PLO's cause with that of the people "to the point of feeling that its salvation was also the people's" (Elias Sambar), the incompetent bureaucratic caste is mainly responsible for the slow slide from unrealistic radicalism to minimalist haggling that leaves out of the reckoning the refugees in Jordan, Syria, and, especially, in the Lebanon, where the feeling of betrayal and abandonment weighing over the camps is turning into pure desperation. Who today remembers the victims of the horrors of Tel al-Zaatar, of the corpses from the massacres in Sabra and Shatila so eloquently described by Jean Genet, the horrors of the siege and crushing of Beirut by Tsahal artillery and aviation? Threatened with expulsion from the heroic *mukhayamat* and martyred on the altar of grandiose projects for the reconstruction of the capital, clinging to the derisory, pathetic property titles of their land and houses lost in 1948, Palestinian refugees in the Lebanon today suffer from being rejected by a society that will not allow them to integrate and from having no aid or help beyond the charity of UNWRA whose aid many question. Three hundred fifty thousand human beings reduced to the status of rubbish from a history of blood and fire, mere sound and fury! The international community shrugs its shoulders: dramas that go on too long become boring.

Yitzhak Rabin's insistence that the PNA should solemnly abrogate the articles of the National Charter that reject the existence of a Jewish state in Palestinian terrritory, as the PLO leader agreed to in Oslo, goes beyond an anachronistic guarantee of security: Arafat had already renounced them in 1988 and in the present situation they only exist on paper. As Israeli professor Amnon Raz Krakotzkin has seen very clearly ("A Peace without History," *Revue d'études palestiniennes,* winter 1995), "what Israel wishes to obliterate is not the texts but the historical consciousness that inspired them, namely Palestinian memory in general. This demand is equivalent to ordering the Palestinians to respect the Zionist conception of history." In other words: the unconditional surrender of national consciousness and abolition of its memory as a complement to teaching a history of Jewish colonization that completely ignores the existence of the Palestinians and reinforces the image of an empty country: to the cry of "a land without people for a people without a land."

It is futile to point out that this pretension will never be accepted by the Palestinians, whose suffering, bitterness, and humiliation has on the contrary sharpened a clear perception of their identity and the injustice of which they are victims.

It is at the moment of its military, political, and economic victory that Israel runs the risk of failure. By sustaining the settlements in Gaza and the West Bank, torpedoing Arafat's PNA, putting off the electoral calendar that had been agreed upon and thus extending Tsahal's military presence in Palestinian cities, and so on, Yitzhak Rabin revealed a surprising lack of political acumen and courage. Time is not necessarily on his side nor is demography: the conversion of tens of thousands of Palestinians into members of Hamas and their readiness to multiply the number of suicide attacks can never be fought by electrified fences or a separation that is impossible because of the capillary crisscrossing created by the uninterrupted colonization of the West Bank. Instead of holding a hand out to the adversary by recognising the Palestinians' right to self-determination and decent living conditions, the stubborn refusal not to yield an inch of what had been gained by force of arms only poisons a conflict which could be resolved through greater magnanimity and vision of the future. The total lack of understanding and respect for the dignity of the Palestinians suggests permanent discord that will in turn perpetuate "the *intifada* by other means," and be harsher and bloodier.

Are Palestinians and Israelis condemned to destroy each other physically and morally for years and for decades? Real agreements for peace and coexistence, like the ones reached by Mandela and de Klerk in South Africa, show how the bitterest struggles can be resolved by generosity, forgiveness, and a sense of history. Years ago, in my 1988 Palestinian diary, I quoted the words of an intellectual from East Jerusalem about the double dream of the descendants of Isaac and Ishmael: the disappearance or nonexistence of the other. But the problem, he concluded, "as much for ourselves as for them, rests in knowing whether we are prepared to accept something less than our dream."

After Oslo, the Israelis cherished the hope that they had realized their dream at the expense of the Palestinians' nightmare. This hope can now be seen to be totally illusory. Only recognition of Palestinian identity and the Palestinian right to an independent, democratic state will one day put an end to the tragedy in the Middle East.

CHECHNYA

THE SUFI BROTHERHOODS

The high-technology digital murder of pro-Independence president Dzhokhar Dudayev, victim of an air-to-land missile
guided by satellite telephone communication while he was
talking to Russian mediator and Duma deputy Constantin
Voronoi, clearly belongs to the gangsterish logic of Yeltsin's
recently purged retinue and he now joins the already long list
of Chechen political-religious leaders or guides, executed or
killed in Russian prisons before and after the Revolution. Imam
Mansur Ushurma, the fiery preacher of holy war against the
conquest of the Caucasus, perished in 1793 in the Tsarist
fortress of Schlöselburg; Kunta Hadji, today venerated as a
guide by the *murid* fighters of Chechnya, was snuffed out in
1867 in one of Alexander II's dungeons; among the successors
to Imam Shamil in the *naqshbandiya silsila* (the initiatory
chain) who did not lay down their weapons, sheik Abdelrrahman of Sogratl, leader of the 1877 uprising, finished his
days in Siberia; the lieutenants of the *wird*, litany of the Batal
Hadji, perished in prison or were deported in the last decades
of the nineteenth century. After the October Revolution and
the ephemeral emirate in the northern Caucasus, the Soviets
executed all the *naqshbandiya* and *kadiri* sheiks who did not
fall in combat: Najmuddin of Gotso and the pro-Independence
chieftains in the 1921–1923 war, captured in 1925 in the
Caucasian Mountains, were killed in cold blood; the leader Ali
Mitraev, son of the founder of the Bamat Giray *wird*, suffered
the same fate in spite of being nominally integrated into the
Chechen Revolutionary Committee created by the Bolsheviks;
all the instigators of the 1930 rebellion, although amnestied by
a peace accord like the one signed on June 10, were executed
the following year. Soviet historian A. M. Tutayev mentions
that five of the six children and eight grandchildren—apart
from the countless cousins, nephews, and sons-in-law—of
the "bandit" Batal Bolhoroiev died in arms or were mercilessly
liquidated. The only survivor, Kurayich, sustained an anti-

Soviet guerrilla unit until 1947, the date of his capture and deportation. The last *abrek* (honorable bandit) who was a solitary thorn in the side of the occupier, protected by the rest of the population and whom the review *Zhurnalist* blamed for the death of forty "patriots" during the era of Kruschev and Brezhnev, fell in a trap, like Dudayev, in 1980 (see the work by Bennigsen and Lemercier-Quelquejay, as well as the latter's articles in *Les voies d'Allah*, Paris 1996).

The symbolic success of the enemy leader's destruction after the disasters and humiliations suffered by the army may have contributed to the spectacular increase in Yeltsin's popularity and satisfied the desire for revenge of the high command of the armed forces and the Russian president's circle of allies defenistrated by Alexander Lebed, but it has far from resolved—quite the contrary—the causes of the conflict. Following in the footsteps of his Tsarist and Soviet predecessors, Yeltsin shut the door on an honorable solution, caught in the dilemma of a retreat that would offend the pan-Slavic electorate or total extermination of the *Chechen cockroaches* (thus spake Pavel Grachov).

Kill the dog and you'll cure the rabies, runs the proverb. But Chechen rage stoked by two centuries of war, *scorched earth* tactics, massive deportations, and summary executions will not be finished off by a single death. To judge by the reaction of his successor and the military leaders, it has, on the contrary, grown in intensity. The grimly wrought chain of executions and extermination in dungeons and Siberian camps of imams and guides is the symbol of their long, ever-defensive struggle against the invader's incursions and savagery. The stubborn thistle, crushed by the cart, in Tolstoy's novel, grows green shoots, does not surrender.

The amnesia of the present Russian leaders in these critical moments of ideological confusion and identity crises— manifested, for example, in Zyuganov's election campaign, his references to Christ and Stalin, quotations from the *Apocalypse*, and free distribution at political meetings of the anti-Semitic pamphlet, spawned by the Tsarist police, *The Protocol of the Elders of Zion*—translates into a loss of historical memory condemning them to repeat the crimes and errors of an idealized, fallacious past. The Chechens, on the other hand, preserve their own carefully, transmit it from generation to generation like a precious treasure. Most significant, when circumstances forced the ending of holy war and the practice of *ketman* (apparent submission), the fighting spirit survived in the *abrelik* or bandits of honor. The *abreks*, like the *morisco* Monfi, keep alive the flame of combat, a reminder that the spirit of resistance has not been extinguished, that the slightest spark may set it alight again. "A Chechen," I was told by a *murid* of Zakan Yurt, "is born with the sign of death inscribed on his forehead. He knows that one day or the next he will die weapon in hand. It is his fate, and from childhood he prepares for the day when his spirit will join the assembled ranks of his forefathers."

The role played by the Sufi brotherhoods in Russian history is much more important than is generally recognised. On the one hand, as the authors of the work quoted point out: "The wars in the Caucasus contributed to the moral and material downfall of the Tsarist empire and precipitated the demise of the Romanov dynasty and the establishment of the Bolshevik regime"; on the other, they created the opposite situation to that caused by the invasion and colonization of Muslim countries in Africa and Asia by the great European powers throughout the nineteenth century and first half of the twentieth: while in the majority of the former, the colonizers safely channeled official Islam, reduced and even marginalized the Sufi brotherhoods, the contrary phenomenon obtained in the USSR. Decimated by the Bolsheviks or entirely subordinated to the Soviet regime, official Islam was absorbed by the brotherhoods and became the backbone of what Soviet specialists described as *parallel Islam*. Despite relentless repression and destruction of mosques—more than nine hundred in the territory of the present republics of Ingushetia and Chechnya in 1917 and only nine in 1984— Sufism did not decline. From the end of the eighteenth century, the defense of religion became part of the preservation and survival of the national community.

The hostility of the Soviet regime toward the rebels did not pardon the dead: when Chechens were deported to Kazhakstan, their cemeteries were razed and the tops or "witnesses" of their tombs used in Russia as building material or as decoration. Those in existence at present date from the return to the country at the end of the fifties. In the districts in the center and south, I managed to inspect half a dozen: sepulchres are dominated by stone or wooden stelas, painted in bright colors—blue, green, white—with a small two-sided roof under a crescent moon. Some reproduce in Arabic the name of Allah or choruses of the *fatiha*. Others, the name and patronym of the deceased and their dates of birth or death.

The *mazars* or hermitages erected in memory of a *mujahid* (martyr) or holy person are the equivalent of the marabouts in the popular Islam of North Africa. Members of the brotherhoods and the faithful gather around them to recite their litanies and beg for their grace. The antireligious persecution suffered in Chechnya up to Gorbachov centered on them: most were flattened and replaced by "anti-obscurantist," atheist propaganda centers. But, at the slightest lapse on the part of the authorities, they suddenly reappeared and drew crowds of pilgrims, including many members of the Communist Party!

The Soviet press in recent decades abounds in descriptions and denunciations of these "focal points of reactionary propaganda" manipulated by "vagabonds," "parasites," and "criminals." The most popular pilgrimages were those to the tombs of Uzun Hadji and Kunta Hadji's mother, in the village of Vedeno. When I met up with the *murids* of Zakan Yurt, I was able to compare the list given by Bennigsen and Lemercier-Quelquejay with the ones they had memorized: the differences were minimal. The *murids* were unaware that foreign researchers took an interest in them and wrote about their struggle and asked me to pass on their prayers and gratitude.

If the *naqshbandiya tarika* embodies the history of Chechen resistance in the last century, the *kadiria* undoubtedly dominates the struggle today. Founded by Abdelkadir Yilani in the twelfth century, the brotherhood gradually spread throughout the entire Islamic world, from China to

Morocco. Their presence in the Caucasus only goes back as far as the nineteenth century and is crystalized in the charismatic figure of Kunta Hadji, whose mystical preaching attracted numerous mountain patriots and disoriented *murids* after Shamil's defeat. Unlike the silent *zikr* of the *naqshalandis*, Kunta Hadji introduced the vocal *zikr*, sometimes accompanied by music and dance: his legend and mysterious death—his disciples even today deny he ever died—confer on him the authority of *spiritual pole* of the northern Caucasus.

Osman Imaiev, Chechnya's ex-public prosecutor, received an entirely Soviet education and continued his studies in the University of Moscow, where he learned to speak correct Spanish. He now resides in the vilage of Kulari and maintains close links with the independence fighters; harboring no great hopes of any outcome, he keeps a record of the war crimes of the occupation force and shares the life of the members of the *kadiri* of Kunta Hadji. He himself confesses to being a novice in the matter, but coordinates the activities of the *murids* and, as I soon see, organizes its ceremonies.

"The *zikr*," he tells me, "is the symbol of Chechen resistance. On 5 September 1995, the Russians were about to enter the village but at the sight of the *murids* praying and dancing on the bridge by the entrance, they gave up their attempt. They know from experience that to attack us would lead to uprisings in many other villages."

The conversation unfolds in a large shed, with a canteen, kitchen, and a dormitory with bunk beds, veiled by a rough curtain, where a dozen rebels on active service spend their nights. The members of the brotherhood gradually arrive and each group of newcomers hums a traditional canticle "to drive the devil away"—a kind of compulsory greeting from the stranger crossing the threshold of a home: they are members of the Kunta Hadji brotherhood of the village of Zakan Yurt.

After introductions and greetings, we head for the mosque: a new, carpeted building, with a niche that serves both as *mimbar* and *qibla*, a wall clock, and two framed pictures of pilgrimages to Mecca. Those present, including my host, crouch down in a circle next to the *mirab:* I am offered a small stool but prefer to make myself comfortable on the floor and observe the spectacle from there. I have attended *kadiri* prayers in Morocco and Egypt and in Sarajevo the week preceding the NATO bombing and the end of the siege. The Chechens possess an emotional intensity which, as many Soviet Islamologist-police point out, moves even the incredulous and the irreverent.

Once the circle is closed, the *murids* wearing their caps initiate prayers and litanies, gently shaking their bodies. First the *wird* (the prayer in honor of Kunta Hadji), the *tahlil* ("God is the one and only god"), and then the solemnly entoned *fatiha*, that seems to soar upward, to spread out with the fervorous resonance of a Gregorian chant. The guide of the brotherhood in the village, the *turji*, signals a pause: the participants exchange greetings and collect themselves in the *nazma* (prayer) before proceeding to the phase of gradual ascent. Reciter and chorus repeat the loudest chant, voices rising like moans from the backs of their throats. Suddenly they begin clapping their hands rhythmically, *la ilaha illa llah*, ever more vigorously, more proudly, stand, go round, counterclockwise, slowly, more rapidly, accelerating, still beating their palms, their spontaneous prayers echo and vibrate in the air, fill the mosque with a sonorous stream of sound. Suddenly, they halt, crouch down, start prayers and preparatory invocations to Kunta Hadji. Osman Imaiev and the older men who are not part of the *zikr* remove their mats, and after a quiet, delicate, absorbed pause, the ceremony enters a new stage. The *murids* begin dancing, now right to left—a novel departure in Islam—run, jump, never interrupting the rhythm of their short prayers, in tighter and tighter circles, each grazing the back of their companion, noisily beating the ground with the soles of their feet. One leaves the circle, gyrates more swiftly than the rest, his magnetic power driving them on, as if invested with mysterious Aeolian energy: first, commander Yacub, then, a bearded youth wearing a black tunic, in an elfin or genie hat out of a fairy story illustration. His energy transforms the circle into a dizzy merry-go-round. Bare feet resound deafeningly on the raised platform, combined with prayers, leaping, and running in circles, reaching a point of suspension when the *murid* is detached from all around, in the words of the greatest Spanish mystic, "without place in understanding, solace in will, language in memory."

When the rite is over, the members crouch in another circle, recite individually and in chorus "God is the one and only god" and tell the ninety-nine beads of their rosaries. Some two hours have passed since I entered, but time has stood still. Meanwhile the sky has cleared, stars shine, and for the first time since I arrived in Chechnya, I hear birdsong. Unashamedly I can affirm: I levitated in an sea of serenity. Not a moment of exaltation or a fleeting eclipse of the senses: it was this moment's beauty, its perfection. Didn't such melodious song in the silence of that night, if only for a few seconds, compensate for the accumulated barbarism?

The bird went quiet, the order of the world returned: in a landscape of war, I lived history's cruel, sordid repetitions.

"GOOD-BYE TO YOU, FOUL LAND OF THE RUSSIAN"

The seesaw history of Russian intervention in Chechnya over almost two centuries has generated a bibliography of publications that is small in number but high in quality. In the first reference work on the subject, *The Russian Conquest of the Caucasus*, J. F. Baddely provides a detailed exposition of Tsarist expansion southward and the atrocities of colonial war against the Islamized mountain peoples a century before. General Yermolov, commander-in-chief of the imperial army between 1816 and 1827—whose statue presided over the main square in Grozny until its demolition in 1990—had suggested, like ex-defense minister Pavel Grachov, purely and simply eliminating the "Chechen bandits." The mountain people's tenacious resistance, stiffened by the Sufi brotherhoods—in particular the *naqsbandiya* and the *kadiria*—lasted from the second decade of the nineteenth century to 1859, date of the defeat and exile to Turkey of Imam Shamil. The *murids* or members of the brotherhoods, described by the soldiers, civil servants, and chroniclers of the period in very similar terms to those used by the "democratic" spokesmen and courtiers of Boris Yeltsin, fought stubbornly for their independence and then suffered the devastating effects of the "scorched earth" policy now openly enforced by the masters of the Kremlin.

Alexandre Benningsen's *Le soufi et le commissaire* is another striking book drawing in its turn an exhaustive portrait of the *turuk* (plural of *tarika*, brotherhood), which weld together and embody the will to survive of a people of just over a million souls confronted by an enemy of infinitely superior resources. The Chechens' expert knowledge of the terrain, spirit of sacrifice, cult of *yigit* (bravery) and practice of *zikr*—collective exaltation and ecstatic dances which so shock and disturb the invader—allowed them to survive and retain their identity by alternating holy war with *ketman*—concealment and apparent submission—while waiting for circumstances favorable to taking up arms, as happened after the 1917 Revolution, when they proclaimed the independence of the Emirate of the northern Caucasus under the authority of an old *naqshbandiya* imam.

Although the rebellion was finally crushed in 1924, the *murids* spread their influence over the neighboring peoples of Ingushetia and Daghestan, and their anti-Soviet guerrilla warfare, despite the systematic destruction of "nests of bandits" and execution of their leaders, lasted until the great purges of 1936 and the Nazi invasion, when the entire Chechen people was deported to Asia.

The nineteenth-century wars in the Caucasus—Imam Shamil's and the one that followed between 1864 and 1877, headed by Kunta Hadji, the *kadiri* or "guide," had a disastrous impact within Russian society: like the invasion of Afghanistan a century later, they provoked the discontent of ordinary people, tired of sending their sons to the slaughterhouse, and sowed a spirit of doubt and self-criticism among a small but select minority of officers and soldiers who had taken part. The creation of a paramilitary body of Cossacks against the "Chechen bandits" was an expedient thought up by the Tsarist command to avoid the dangerous consequences of exhaustion and defeatism among the population. After Shamil Basayev's daring incursion into Budennovsk in June 1995, we see the rehabilitation and reactivation of that corps, impregnated with traditionalist mysticism and hatred for the peoples of the Caucasus, and abolished seventy years earlier because they collaborated with the White Russians during the civil war.

With the collapse of the USSR and the fresh proclamation of Chechen independence by General Dudayev, the cycle of history is repeated: the past becomes present once more, though its bitter lessons have not been assimilated. If an architect of the "pacification" of Chechnya declared in 1834 "the only thing to be done with these people is to wipe them off the face of the earth," Boris Yeltsin's recent words, "they (the 'bandits') must be exterminated like rabid dogs," demonstrate the longevity of lethal clichés among a broad sector of Russian panSlavic nationalists, for which "a Chechen can only kill; and if he can't kill, he's a bandit and a robber; and if he finds that too much, he's a petty thief; and if not, then he's no Chechen" (from statements by General Barsukov, one of Yeltsin's favorites, as recorded by the correspondent of *El País,* 21 January 1996). It is futile to add that the use and abuse of such language ominously prefigures recourse to a "final cleansing."

The epic misfortune of these mountain peoples caught the attention and sympathy of various Russian writers in the nineteenth century. In their youth, they had left as volunteers, in search of adventure, or were sent forcibly to "pacify" the Caucasus where they acquired firsthand knowledge of the facts and the fighting spirit of those apparently "pacified." Of the more or less fictionalized testimonies, two by great writers stand out: Mikhail Lermontov (1814–1841) and Leon Tolstoy (1828–1910). The events described in their stories present a lively scenario of prejudices, emotions, sympathies, and admiration for the enemy, in a word, the contradictory emotions they generated in their authors. Lermontov's romantic rebellion against Russian authoritarianism is a long way from the more reflective and consequently more incisive, more devastating outlook from the elderly Tolstoy's retrospective vantage point.

In the brief narrative entitled *Bela,* the first chapter of his novel *A Hero for Our Time,* Lermontov displays a reasonable knowledge of the lands recently incorporated into the empire and the chivalresque legends of its inhabitants. He sprinkles his prose—as does Tolstoy—with words and phrases from the Caucasian languages—originating mainly from Arabic and Turkish—and carefully differentiates the ethnic components of the region: not only Chechens, but also Osettians, Cherkeses, Kalabardins, Tartars, either already subject to the Russian conqueror or exiled in Ottoman territory. The plot of *Bela* is woven round the dialogue between the narrator and a veteran of the Caucasian wars who, sheltering in a primitive, ramshackle inn, relates in fits and starts the story of the capture of Bela by Pechorin, the story's hero, and the dramatic end to their joint adventure, resolved by bullets according to the code of tribal honor. Many of the ingredients of this chapter evoke in Spanish readers the *morisco* novel, *The Civil Wars in Granada* by Ginés Pérez de Hita or Calderón's *Tuzani de la Alpujarra*, which combine contempt for the enemy with idealization, against a blackcloth of oriental or Moorish exoticism, paying implicit homage to the temerity and character of a people defeated by the superior knowledge and weapons of the "civilizer."

The figure of the veteran is using already hackneyed language to refer to the Chechens and other rebel peoples: "descamisados" who ambush the army and "give us a wretched time," since one never knows, he says, if lurking in the rocky terrain, "one of those shaggy devils is spying on you." In fact, the old soldier serves the poet's purpose by expressing his compatriots' usual point of view in respect to the "Asiatic" enemy, like some of Cervantes's characters who voice the common opinions of old Christians:

> These Asiatics are such cunning rogues. Do you think they're driving their oxen with those shouts? How the devil do you know what they're shouting? But the oxen understand them. If you want, you can order them to yoke up twenty oxen; though while they shout at the oxen in their language, they won't budge. They're terrible thieves. But what can one do? They like fleecing travellers. We haven't taught these ruffians any better. You see how they'll soon be asking me for money for vodka. I know them too well. They won't trick me.

Despite the negative value judgment—shared by many Russians today—the veteran is unable to hide his astonishment at the rebels' spirit of belicose defiance: "It's difficult to put these bandits down. I've seen some of them in action, still swinging their sabres, though they're stuck full of bayonet holes like a sieve."

Obviously, the hard-bitten soldier does not ponder the reasons for the suicidal heroism of Imam Shamil's *murids*. Nor does Lermontov. The times didn't encourage that kind of question. But, in order to lay bare the great poet's state of mind it would be better to put aside his Cossack cradle song with its clichéd reference to the "Chechen bandit" and dwell on his startling curse and imprecation against a stepmother homeland: a composition that still captivates and enthralls today's readers, stunned by Lermontov's onslaught against the enslavement of bodies and souls by the perennial author-itarianism of the Russian tradition:

> Goodbye to you, foul
> Land of the Russian,
> Nation of masters
> And slaves.
> Goodbye to the blue-dyed
> Uniforms,
> Goodbye to the people they
> Manacle.
>
> Perhaps behind the
> High Caucasus,
> I can hide from your
> Tyrants,
> From eyes that see
> All,
> From ears that miss
> Nothing.

(translation from Antonio Pérez-Ramos's Spanish version)

The stories and eyewitness accounts of those mobilized by a "foul" land, published in the fragile, threatened independent Russian press, bristle with similar bitterness and anger. The treatment suffered by the country after the collapse of the USSR and its conversion by legal sleight-of-hand and devious stratagems to "democratic values and the market economy" has meant, in a sudden shock, the shattering of all dreams, the usurping of the power vacuum by cabbals and cliques, the destruction of their standard of living by galloping infla-tion, a steep fall in production, untrammeled speculation, scenes of Dickensian poverty, drunks with extremities ampu-tated because of frostbite, old people thrown out of their homes, gangsters, sharks, mafiosi warfare. All that has arisen after the dashing of ephemeral hopes of change and the reduction of public freedoms to the freedom of the gambling casino run by seven-lived *apparatchiks* and fake entrepre-neurs of the "Chicago School" defended by awesome, only too real bodyguards, have sapped civic morale and led the Russian Federation to the edge of the abyss.

Like Lermontov, many young people berate the despot's slaves and courtiers, curse the uniforms of army and police, now differently colored but equally arbitrary. Russia at the end of the millennium recalls many features of the country subjected in the nineteenth century to the masters of the imperial *ukase*. What fearful redeemer or messiah will appear to save her?

TOLSTOY AND WAR IN THE
CAUCASUS: *HADJI MURAD*

Tolstoy endured the war in the Caucasus from 1851 to 1853 as a state functionary and artillery officer. The depth and lasting nature of this experience can be measured in the work he began writing more than four decades later, knowing full well it would never pass the censors. The intervening years enabled him to decant his early ideas and emotions and gave him a more profound historical understanding of events, after the second and equally bloody "pacification" of Chechnya. A mature work, written and corrected in bursts during the author's old age, *Hadji Murad* would not see the light until after his death. The first Russian edition of 1912 suffered the scissor snips and excisions of the fearful surgeons of ideas: the unabridged text had to be published in Berlin.

Skimming the pages of this story is extremely enlightening for anyone who has closely followed the events in Chechnya from the proclamation of independence by General Dudayev to military intervention "for a few hours" in December 1994 and the new, interminable "pacification": it generates an in-depth vision of the events that one reads about daily in the press and these in turn impregnate the reading of the text with a painful, provocative impression of present reality.

Tolstoy draws a sober portrait, making no concessions to patriotic tub-thumping, of the Russian conquest of the Caucasus, around the seductive, contradictory figure of Hadji Murad, Imam Shamil's lieutenant — whose fleeting desertion to the Russians and death at their hands after a frustrated escape attempt is based on a real incident, supported by historical sources. The brutality of Tsarist repression against the iron resistance of the Chechens, the rivalries in the corridors of power and the contradictory tactics, grotesque triumphalism, incompetence of the generals, and the corruption of leaders and officers are mercilessly delineated. So, we learn that "the brilliant feat of the Russian army" celebrated by the press is in reality a Chechen ambush in which dozens of soldiers perished, heroically killed "defending the Tsar, the Fatherland and Orthodox Faith."

While he unfurls his beautiful narrative of his hero's surrender and gilded captivity, the writer describes the military in an aside as "thieves and brigands," in the words of one officer, capable of selling their weapons to the rebels to pay off their gambling debts; he mentions the existence of officers who appropriate money destined for the troops and of a colonel threatened with a court-martial for fraud in the course of supplying the regiment; he points out the devastation wrought by vodka and embezzlement by those responsible for administration; he outlines a somber, grotesque picture of the pyramid of general corruption from top to bottom. Like Yeltsin, the great Nicholas I was convinced that in this "pyramid of functionaries mounted on the people and against the people," graphically described today by Serguei Kovaliov, everybody was stealing. 'He knew it was essential to punish the thieves and hoodlums but equally that it wouldn't prevent those who came in their stead from doing exactly the same. Stealing was the wont of functionaries, his duty as Tsar was to sanction them and, however fastidiously, he carried out his line of action perfectly." Could one find a description that better matched with amazing continuity the one given today by the official foreign correspondents in Moscow and the organs of the independent Russian press yet to be silenced by the new Tsar's censorship?

Nicholas I's audience with Chernishov, his minister of War— any similarity with Pavel Grachov or the ineffable Mikhail Barsukov is purely coincidental!—gives Tolstoy the opportunity to re-create the atmosphere of crawling, supine adulation surrounding the autarch: the worth of his advisers and confidants was measured, as now, by the degree of curvature to the spine as they bow and their blind obedience to his fickle, contradictory orders. Again, the reader thinks he is watching scenes performed by contemporary actors: airy promises of peace offered up to the honest people interspersed with threats of extermination, according to the moods of the despot:

the servility of his retinue—continuous, glaring, flying in
the face of evidence—led him to the extreme of not seeing his own contradictions, of not tempering his words
and deeds with reality, logic or even common sense; he
was convinced that all his dispositions, however sense-
less, unjust and mutually opposed, were sensible, just
and well-balanced simply because they were his.

Nicholas I's programme—the razing of dwellings, the
destruction of crops, and relentless harassing of the bandits—
was carried out to the letter:

Not a single inhabitant was left in the village. The soldiers carried orders to set fire to the corn, to the hay
and even to the *saklyas* (houses). An acrid smell spread
over the whole settlement and shrouded the soldiers
who grabbed everything they found in the houses,
trapped and shot dead the chickens the mountain people hadn't been able to take with them.

Better informed than Lermontov as to the religious-patriotic
nature of Chechen resistance, Tolstoy paints in firm brus
strokes the proselytism of the *murids* and their preaching of
gazauet or holy war in the villages of neighboring Daghestan
but, curiously, does not note their support for the principles
and rules of the vast and as yet intact *naqshbandiya* brotherhood whose guide was Shamil. The portrait he draws of the
latter isn't at all flattering: his authoritarianism, like General
Dudayev's 140 years later, fed the discontent of one sector of
his people and fostered desertions like that of the story's hero
but his status as spiritual leader and strict application of the
sharia drew around him all the mountain people unwilling to
accept the imperial logic and the benefits of Russian-style
"civilizing" progress. The "criminals, Mafiosi, terrorists and
murderers" regularly denounced by Yeltsin and Grachov —
who should be eradicated "like a cancerous tumour" by
massive bombing raids, multiple rocket missile launchers,
artillery attacks, "scorched earth" tactics, and assault by the

elite corps—are the descendants of these Chechens admirably portrayed by Tolstoy's righteous pen:

> The old people had gathered in the square, and crouched down, assessed the situation. Nobody spoke of hatred towards the Russians. What Chechens felt, young and old alike, was stronger than hatred. Not hatred but disgust, repulsion, confusion at the senseless cruelty of those Russian dogs, and the desire to exterminate them as rats are exterminated or poisonous spiders and wolves, in a word, a feeling as natural as the instinct for self-preservation.

The moral outrage of personalities like Serguei Kovaliov, ex-head of the Commission for Human Rights attached to the presidency, of Yelena Bonner, Sakharov's widow, and of numerous intellectuals and democrats can thus take strength from Tolstoy's undeniable authority and his lasting influence on the Russian people. *Hadji Murad* in no way belongs to the catalog of pamphlets denouncing the iniquities of colonialism; it is an excellent narrative, subtle, layered, giving space to the different protagonists in the conflict: to oppressors and oppressed, to officers seduced by the primitive life and customs of the Caucasus—like Buttler, probably the author's alter ego—and to characters full of hidden crannies, as enigmatic as the man who gives the book its title. The ballad sung to Hadji Murad by one of his loyal followers, with its lilting, painful invocation of death, constitutes one of the most moving passages in this short but richly textured work.

With the revolution of 1917, the Chechens rallied to Lenin's promises of liberation for the peoples subjected by the Tsarist yoke. But the emirate of the northern Caucasus was soon denounced, fought, and crushed as in the days of Shamil and Kunta Hadji. From 1924, the struggle against the "bandits" and "fanatics," barely mentioned in the press, was implacably carried into the middle of the following decade. There is no literary account: only official propaganda and internal documents of the army and security organizations. After the massive deportation of the Chechens to Kazakhstan on 23 February 1944, we hear of them, thanks to pages in Solzhenitsyn's third volume of *The Gulag Archipelago*. The shared experience in the camps came to life in an admiring portrait of this Caucasian people united in adversity and hardened by more than a century of struggles, despite his raw description of their clannish customs and revenge of family honor that thirty years of Sovietization had failed to uproot:

> But there was a nation [in the *gulag*] that never yielded, never adopted the mental habit of submission—not just a bunch of rebels but the entire nation.—I mean the Chechens. . . . [They] never sought to please, to flatter the camp bosses; their attitude was haughty and, in fact, openly hostile [. . .] Something extraordinary must be mentioned. No-one could stop them from living the way they lived. The regime which had governed the land for three decades could not force them to respect its laws.

After the return to the Caucasus in the Kruschev era, the embers of the fire of independence remained covered in ash: a long period of *ketman* in which the *kadiri* Sufis kept their secret structures intact. Today, the flames spread anew and the stupid cruelty of history is repeated. Shamil Basaiev and Salman Raduiev, solitary wolves and grandsons of Imam Shamil, seem as if wrenched from the pages of Lermontov and Tolstoy. Also Dudayev's attacks on the "nest of bandits" have a familiar ring in our ears: they refer to the village of Vedeno, Imam Shamil's bastion and refuge.

Tolstoy's work opens and closes with a detailed description of a wild thistle with crimson flowers. The narrator's persistent attempts to cut and tie them in a nosegay are both arduous and futile. Its stem pricks like a hedgehog, the fiber is coarse and stiff, and his attempts to behead it end in disaster.

"Sorry I'd destroyed such a beautiful flower," he writes, "I threw it down. But what strength! what vital energy! I thought to myself as I remembered the effort it had taken to uproot it. How it defends itself, how dearly it sold its life!"

The truncated thistle, with its mutilated stumps, broken stems, and blackened flower, crushed by the weight of an armored car, is the first image that comes to the mind of the traveler stepping foot in Chechnya: but the thistle has raised itself up again and, though damaged and battered, stands firm. As Tolstoy noted perceptively, its sap never surrenders.

TSAR BORIS

As one leaves Moscow's international airport, the rapid transformation of the urban landscape over the last five years confuses and bewilders. On the new motorway leading to the capital, advertisements for Stella Artois and Marlboro hang from the lampposts welcoming travelers. They soon give way to advertisements for Fuji, Lucky Strike, Samsung, Campari, Camel, and other Russian and Western products. But, as the taxi turns into the city, the advertising hype is eclipsed by huge, ubiquitous posters, plastered along avenues and boulevards. Boris Yeltsin, in impeccable statesmanlike garb, is shaking hands with Yuri Luzhkov, the popular, populist mayor of Moscow, who has efficiently *cleansed* the city center of beggars and undesirables, reduced street insecurity without touching a hair of the mafia, exerted iron control over inhabitants of Caucasian origins, built big blocks of flats for the middle classes, and completed the brand-new ring of motorways now surrounding the capital. The silhouettes of the president and mayor, superimposed on a background of Kremlin walls and golden church domes, are thus endowed with the respect and magnetic power of the symbols of absolute power and the national church, a faithful servant for centuries to the aristocracy and Tsarist imperial expansion.

The 1990 scenes of abject misery are less visible: the mayor has swept them under the carpet. Now the poverty-stricken 80 percent of the Russian population languishes in the huge periphery of ruined factories and dismantled industries. However, brutal contrasts remain: the former Gum state department stores, in Red Square, have been colonized by French perfumes and the United Colors of Benetton. Their customers are clones of those in any Western city. Russian executives with their obligatory black briefcases imitate the dress style of North American colleagues, but their appearance and manners of the newly free, newly rich betrays a novice status: like the girls who adorn the thoroughfares of the center, they imitate the gestures and tics of the models portrayed in *Cosmopolitan* yet retain traces of the back of beyond: they are the *new Russians*. Hours later, I glimpse them on television disguised as tennis players, with the attributes of golfers, sweaty, clumsy, lunging with their rackets or blindly lashing out at the ball a few meters from the elusive, mocking hole that represents their yearning for respectability and life at the top. As General Alexander Lebed wrote — one of the candidates in the presidential election, before his recent investiture as successor by Yeltsin to ensure his own victory in the second round of the elections:

> 'In Russia there are practically two governments. One with an aged president . . . and another with an entirely different structure, harsher and more determined. We have millions of needy people on wretchedly small pensions and no reward for their lifetime's work. But the criminals enjoy their Mercedes, their villas, their holidays in the Canary Islands. The government levies taxes on businessmen and the Mafia also gets its slice from those who don't want to fly through the air in their cars. . . . How can an honest person survive in a country like this? (*Moscow Times*, 1 June 1996)

The move from the foyer and lounges of the Hotel M.— their foreign and Russian guests partners in the greedy purchase of ruinous state enterprises, tables and sofas occupied by imposing bodyguards, chamber music concerts played by a quartet in gleaming wigs and eighteenth-century costume — to the hustle and bustle in the parks and spaces by the nearby metro station comes as a shock to anyone who visited the capital in the glorious, now distant times of the "construction of socialism."

At dusk after the long days of a Russian summer, the pensioners and victims of reconversion to the market economy and dizzy collapse of the roble line up a short walk away from Red Square and its display of miscellaneous merchandise. In a straight line, with almost barrack-yard discipline, like the good old times in the Soviet Fatherland. If someone steps forward and breaks the line, an improvized, scruffy corporal immediately gives the call to order. The scene reminds me of the first and most beautiful novel by Solzhenitsyn. Grandmothers, old men wearing their pathetic decorations as heroes of labor, functionaries reduced to penury, skinny women in thick socks and slippers, and sickly looking youths offer passersby plastic bags, giant containers of Pepsi-Cola, bottles of suspiciously ill-defined liquid, cheap vodka, bread, cigarettes, the indelible signs of decrepitude and misfortune, rancor and bitterness glazed on their faces.

A little farther on, street sellers hawk newspapers and magazines with portraits of Stalin and nationalist and anti-Semitic pamphlets. Various groups heatedly argue about politics and compare the respective "merits" of the candidatures of Zhirinovski and Zyuganov. Under the archway leading into the square, women with crucifixes round their necks cross themselves and offer their bag for alms. Some parishioners, led by a priest, walk past the newly rebuilt churches opposite the walls of the Kremlin and the Father of the Revolution's closed mausoleum.

Back at the hotel, I follow the details of the election campaign on the Russian television news. The rest of the candidates appear fleetingly, in stingily apportioned slots, but Tsar Boris enjoys magnanimous, attentive, flattering treatment. I duly admire him dancing, flanked by bodyguards, with a pretty, folklorically clad blonde; in his role as generous autarch or Father Christmas, promising miraculous increases in pensions and payment of overdue wages to employees and workers; suddenly, his beady eyes and irritated face harangue a military audience; at a rock concert full of young people, he sways with the feather-light grace of a Jesus Gil amid a group of Atletico Madrid fans. I await the final flourish (a *Swan Lake* to emulate Nureyev?) but sleep wins out and I am left nursing my fantasy.

The vilification and slandering of the criminal-to-be, a key element in Serbian ultranationalist propaganda to justify the genocide of Muslims, has been used to paroxysm point by Yeltsin and his advisers, searching for a scapegoat for his disastrous economic policies, the gangsterization of society and the sinking of the majority of the Russian people into abysses of physical and moral misery which bring to mind those described by Dostoyevski and Gorki. To define the Chechen as "bandit," "criminal," and "mafiosi" justifies the atrocities of a war of extermination against a people that incarnates so much abjection and infamy. As the journalist Yevgueni Ijlov recently wrote: "Russian society has been offered on a plate, most opportunely, the ideal adversary, a combination of 'Caucasian Mafia' and 'Islamic fundamentalist.' A confrontation between 'Russians' and 'Caucasians,' with not the least suggestion of any possible cultural dialogue, leads quickly to a rapid conclusion: the others should disappear from our sight."

Milošević and his Serbo-Bosnian colleagues' recipe to "render the victim suspicious, smear his image, construct a sufficiently murky picture of the enemy in order to avoid disturbing the moral peace of the distant observers" is also, in effect—as Veronique Nahoum-Grappe and Yves Cahen have acutely observed—Yeltsin's and Grachov's. The West, scalded by the turn of events in Afghanistan and erroneously convinced of the need to maintain the Russian president's "democratic gains" en route to a market economy, does not and will not intervene. No one or almost no one will react like Tolstoy's character, Marya Dmitrievna, when she lambasts her fellows after a *cleansing* operation against Imam Shamil's "brigands" in the previously mentioned novel. "What war? You are simply murderers."

But the parallels and similarities between the "democrat" Yeltsin and the Serbian leaders don't stop there: just as Milošević paralysed the workings of the Yugoslav Federation and emptied it of any meaning in order to get rid of its president Ante Marković and launch himself as the leader and paladin of Greater Serbia, Yeltsin used the military plot of August 1991 to dismantle the complex structure of the USSR and liquidate Gorbachov. If we take this comparison further, we discover that Yeltsin also learned a lot from the double-speak of his friends Milošević and Karadžić—recently decorated by him with the Cross of St. Andrew despite his prosecution for war crimes by the Court of The Hague—when he proliferates his blythe promises of harmony while opting for a military solution and completing the devastation of Chechnya.

On the eve of the G-7 summit in Moscow, the Russian president momentarily concealed his bloated *camorra* behind a mask of doelike innocence, in the hope of seducing his guests. The massacres and bombings continued but the old *apparatchik*, skilled in the art of lying knowing you're lying, pulled out his sleeve unexpected plans for peace and improvised promises of truces designed to dazzle ephemerally, with exquisite timing, the Western colleagues on whose aid he depends.

From 27 May, date of the signing of the protocol intended to stop armed confrontation and to lead to the exchange of prisoners with the Chechen delegation headed by President Zelichman Yanderbiev, to the agreement reached in Nazran, in the neighboring Republic of Ingushetia, between the Russian minister for nationalities Viacheslav Mikhailov and the commander-in-chief of the independence fighters Aslan Maschadov—an agreement that foresees the withdrawal of the Federation Army by the end of August and the postponing of Chechen parliamentary elections organised by the puppet regime of Doku Zavgaiev, but leaves out the crucial question of independence—Yeltsin has alternated pacifying and warmongering declarations according to his audience. In keeping with the poker-faced fickleness so well delineated by Tolstoy in his portrait of Nicholas I, he maintains two totally antagonistic positions: he presents himself as a man of peace to his potential young electors and unburdens on the shoulders of his unpopular ex-minister of defense the task of preaching "the crushing of the bandits."

The confusion seemed to clear somewhat on 28 May: after holding the Chechen president as a hostage in Moscow, Yeltsin flew to Ossetia in the north and from there by helicopter to the military airport of Severny, near Grozny, the base of the 205th Motorized regiment. "You have won the war," he told the army leaders and officers. "We have destroyed the criminal regime." Words clearly intended to soothe the fury of the military command, nearly all supporters of Zhirinovski and Zyuganov, on the point of mutiny after his Kremlin encounter with Dudayev's successor. Airily sidestepping the danger (ever airborne!) of his much trumpeted visit to Grozny—in whose entrenched center a small heliport, round like a dance floor, had been hurriedly mounted—the president limited himself to shaking hands with Cossacks in a Chechen village and solemnly proclaiming: "The Republic of Chechnya is in Russia and nowhere else."

Subsequently, while ceasefire agreements like the one he had announced unilaterally on 31 March were ignored and the *special operations* continued, Yeltsin came up with the idea of "broad autonomy" similar to that in Tatarstan and encouraged the planned peace conversations, first in Daghestan—frustrated by the siege of the city of Shali and the murder of the independence leader Rashid Barguishev when he came to negotiate with his besiegers—and then in Ingushetia. But the imperious need to string out talks and avoid new military disasters to animate the presidential campaign finally took shape in the 10 June peace agreement. The numerous concessions to Chechen demands—suspension of the parliamentary elections under Russian control, lifting of the siege of the villages, dismantling the inspection and lookout posts on the roads, were not greeted with inflated expectation by independence leaders. The pacts of 30 July 1995, signed after Shamil Basayev's daring incursion in Budennovsk — which also stipulated the gradual withdrawal of the army and disarming of Chechens, except for the small self-defense groups in the villages—soon became, like Yelstin's later would-be ceasefire, a dismal dead letter. The sustaining of the ersatz parliamentary contest by Zavgaiev's pro-Russian government, in flagrant violation of the agreements, is a first indicative sign of Moscow's continuing double game.

The Russian president's aim to win the elections at any cost forced him to throw in the towel and appear to yield, but what will happen after his probable victory in the second round? Will the Chechens accept the demilitarization of their tiny republic with no more guarantees than the Kremlin master's garrulous moodiness? Will a new game of semantic changes begin like the ones that changed the army's bloody offensives into *special operations* and the sinister internment camps into *filter points?* To up the ante, an eventual victory for Ziuganov, according to many independence fighters, would stiffen the resolve of the most troublesome leaders and officers and aggravate the situation.

The U.S. and European Union backing for the Russian president shows yet again how Western chancelleries will sacrifice democratic principles and human rights on the altar of their own self-interest. Admittance of Russia into the Council of Europe, new loans from the International Monetary Fund, and the visits looking for support from political leaders in Paris, London, Bonn, and Washington reveal deep ignorance of Russian reality and of Yeltsin's role as self-styled herald of the market economy, supporter of democrats and hammer against Communists.

What importance has a small people of just over a million souls whose only crime, now a century old, derives from the mere fact of its existence in the strategic area of a great power with an "imperial vocation"? The IMF continues to finance a war effort costing millions of dollars daily. Is the genocide a purely internal Russian affair and is all condemnation from the outside humiliating, inadmissible interference? The call directed some months ago by Sakharov's widow, Yelena Bonner, to the UN secretary general is aimed against this moral fuzziness and short-sightedness: "Although I don't approve of the tone or style of the (later assassinated) general Dudayev, he is right in the essentials. Responsibility for the new genocide being carried out in Chechnya rests with Yeltsin."

URBICIDE, MASSACRES, AND
MASS GRAVES

On 11 December 1994, the Russian army invaded the Republic of Chechnya "in order to restore constitutional order" and eliminate a regime of "bandits and criminals." According to the ex-minister of defense, Pavel Grachov, the operation was to last a few hours: a simple victory parade. Seventeen months later, the "parade" has brought some forty thousand civilian victims, including numerous Russians installed in Grozny; the losses of the army of occupation stands at around ten thousand dead and posted missing; and the devastation of the capital, smaller settlements, and hamlets can only be compared, in dimension and intensity, to that caused in some Russian and German cities during World War II. In little more than a year and a half of conquest, the army has suffered greater losses than in the twelve years of its disastrous adventure in Afghanistan.

As in Afghanistan, the new Kremlin leaders first tried to disguise the operation as the work of a group of "patriots" resolved to rid themselves of Dudayev's tyranny and corruption. In November 1994, the tanks entered Grozny for the first time under the pretext of "fraternal help" to honest Chechens, but the incursion ended catastrophically. The armored cars were destroyed by grenade throwers and, in spite of official disclaimers from Moscow attributing the outburst to mysterious mercenaries, the Russian military leaders had to swallow the bitter pill of taking charge of the prisoners generously handed back by Dudayev. Neither the painful reminder of the defeat in Afghanistan which contributed so much to the fall of the Soviet regime nor the successive wars against the Chechens from the time of Imam Mansur helped Yeltsin or Pavel Grachov foresee the likelihood that their troops would gradually be bogged down in a quagmire, sucked into a mess they would not escape easily. Hence the pathetic efforts of state television and press to hide the wretched truth, to cover up the barbarism, clumsiness, and disorganization of the military operations, transmuting disasters into heroic actions, rehearsing the ritual litany of the "imminent liquidation of the last bandit hide-outs." Despite so much pigheaded fabrication and self-deception—a legacy of the defunct regime of the USSR—Shamil Basayev's incursions in Budennovsk and Raduyev's in Kiliar, with the victorious return of both to Chechnya in the face of intense fire from the army that inflicted more losses in their own ranks than in the enemy's, opened the eyes of a sector of public opinion and upped the number of citizens opposed to the war. Few, very few reinforcements of undernourished, badly paid soldiers, officers, or petty officers now want to risk their lives and meet a glorious end on the field of honor. Chechnya, clearly, isn't worth the candle.

The proclamation of the independence of this autonomous republic of thirteen thousand square kilometers on 27 October 1991 by the general of the Soviet air force, Dzhokhar Dudayev, is reminiscent in many ways of that made by the *naqshbandiya* Nadjmuddin in Gotso in August 1917, later led militarily by Sheik Uzun Hadji: in both cases their authors took advantage of the opportunities opened up by the collapse of Tsarism and the foreseeable breakup of the USSR. A significant precursor of Dudayev, Kaitmas Alichanov, a colonel of Chechen stock in Nicholas II's army, participated actively in the struggle for independence, first against the Cossacks and Denikin's White Russians and then against the Bolsheviks. The war was exceptionally savage and the *murids*, led by Mohammed of Balkani, whose tomb or *mazar* in Daghestan is the object of pilgrimages in less harsh times than ours, annihilated a whole brigade of the Red Army in the valley of Arkhan, very close to the place where on 15 April this year a convoy of the 245th Motorized Infantry Regiment was wiped out and its complement of tanks burned. The war ended provisionally in 1925 with the capture of Imam Najmuddin and his lieutenants in their mountain fastnesses in the Caucasus. Both today and in the era of Imam Shamil, the villages of Vedeno and Bamut suffered a merciless, bitterly fought siege.

But unlike imam Shamil and the religious leaders of the Emirate of the northern Caucasus, Dudayev did not succeed in winning over to his leadership a clear-cut, determined majority of Chechens. His hereditary concept of the state, the fragmentation of the clans, and his passivity—some say complicity—in relation to the local Mafia aroused discord and set him at odds with various sectors of the independence movement. During the three years of his presidency, Chechnya was thrown into turmoil: scores were settled and corruption flourished. As Osman Imaiev, the Republic's former public prosecutor and member of the delegation that discussed with the Russians the ceasefire of 30 July 1995, admitted to me, a number of files passed through his hands of those "disappeared" in confrontations between rival clans. The laying of the oil pipeline from the Caspian to the Black Sea through Chechen territory equally aroused the greed and latent war of conflicting interests. But what Dudayev failed to achieve through personal maneuvering and weakness, the Russians created in a few days with their brutal intervention in December and devastation of the capital: almost total Chechen unanimity in defense of their independence.

It is no exaggeration to speak of Leningrad or Dresden, and those black-and-white images of desolation forever etched in the memory. The center of Grozny was literally flattened by the joint action of heavy artillery, tank fire, missiles, and bombs launched from airplanes and helicopters. The Presidential Palace from whose cellars Dudayev resisted, Parliament, the Institute of Pedagogical Sciences, the National Bank of the Republic, the Higher Institute for Petroleum Studies, the Abdelrrahman Avturkhanov Museum, the Lermontov Theatre, the Fine Arts Museum, the Caucasus Hotel, and so on all vanished from the face of the earth. To conceal the magnitude of the urbicide, mountains of debris were heaped up and thrown on rubbish tips and pits around Grozny. The infill work proceeds and the authors of the "feat" have erected a veil of metal fences around the affected area to ward off prying eyes. Through cracks and holes one can glimpse even today the incessant activity of bulldozers and crushers. Only a handful of wild shrubs and small trees survive the devastation. On the horizon, two plumes of black smoke top the blazing oil wells on the outskirts: their burning still darkens the gloomy atmosphere and, now and then, the voracious, blazing flames reach up as a living symbol of the hell that descended on the city like a bird of prey.

In neighboring areas the spectacle is, if possible, more desolate: hollowed-out buildings, blackened eye sockets and toothless mouths; wrinkled, half-melted houses, facades pitted by smallpox; derisory traffic signals; ghostly cranes suspended in the void. A pink block of flats, once occupied by the local *nomenklatura,* shows off slightly twisted Doric, Ionic, and Corinthian columns, balconies with singed balustrades, small opera-boxish balconies mushy as meringues. My companion tells me a Russian family survives, crouched in one of the back cellars. We go to have a look: a half-crippled man with a disturbed mother and a nine-year-old girl live in a dingy room exposed to the elements: no work, no wages, no help. They subsist like many old and infirm Russians on Chechen charity. Although the Caucasians keep alive the bonds of family and clan solidarity, the Russians suffer a more tragic destiny, abandoned by the indifference of their compatriots responsible for their plight. The old women begging in the area of the market show that the invaders' destructive fury didn't even spare their compatriots.

In a park by the fenced-off area, among trees and rose borders, I discover the incongruous statue of a bear on a bicycle in what two years ago must have been a children's park. The small monument had had better luck than the one erected to Lenin a hundred meters further on, which only preserves its pedestal. (Days later, in an abandoned plot by the battered railway station, I found an enormous and neglected statue of the Soviet leader, guarded by the thick undergrowth that enveloped him: there, Vladimir Illich Ulyanov seemed to be preaching fiercely and energetically at the leafy vegetation on behalf of a new, equally implacable ecological revolution.)

The rest of the city offers the same scenario of rage and

decrepitude: ruined buildings, burned-out tanks, skeleton roofs, hanging beams, entire districts abandoned by their inhabitants. Sometimes, in the remnant of a building, a sign warns off possible marauders: "People living here" or even more laconically, "People alive." The new city center, with the pro-Russian presidency building and army barracks, is a veritable entrenched battleground: fortified post, tanks at every corner—nests of machine guns on the roofs of main buildings, endless soldiers and policemen on a war footing. All the places I have visited—the press center, the offices where I obtained first my Russian press credentials and, then, those from Zavgaiev's puppet administration—are protected by sandbags and guards with machine guns. Despite such an imposing array of strength, the capital conquered in two months of blood and fire fell in a few hours on 6 March to several hundred independence fighters armed with grenade throwers. As the success of the lightning incursion demonstrates, the much heralded Russian pacification is quite illusory. As I saw for myself days later, night belongs to the Chechens and the innumerable control posts and military bases set up in the theoretically pacified zone are frequently transformed into besieged islets, exposed to sudden thrusts from an invisible enemy force.

To the indeterminate number of civilian deaths caused by the war—Russian and Chechen commentators and experts estimate a figure of forty thousand—must be added the number of people who disappear in regular roundups and are sent to the sinister *filter points.* Together with Ricardo Ortega, Antena 3's Moscow correspondent, I interviewed the Red Cross president in Grozny, Hussein Khamidov. This civil aviation pilot's life abruptly changed direction the day he found the corpses of two of his children in a common grave, a few weeks after they "vanished" at the end of January 1995. Since then, Khamidov, elegantly dressed in grey suit and tie, has devoted himself entirely to the task of uncovering the slaughterhouses and ossuaries scattered throughout Chechen territory and to photographing the victims. Seated in his tiny office, he shows us sheaves of cards with carefully appended photographs.

Each dead person appears marked with a number to the pro-visional figure of 1,313. Four hundred and twenty-six have been identified and numerous people come to his office to search out and identify their relatives. As we talk, a man who has eleven disappeared in his family arrives: he comes daily, hopeful that new "finds" will allow him to bury one of them.

Identification is difficult: in many cases, they are skulls scalped or incinerated by flame-throwers, curled-up corpses stacked in munitions boxes in fetal position. Almost all bear signs of torture and summary execution: shot at close range in eyes, forehead, neck, hands tied by rope or wire. In a piti-less succession of horror prints, I gaze at victims with empty eyesockets, hollow nasal orifices, skulls set in a cast howling, gasping from asphyxiation, protesting indignation, signs of shock, unspeakable pain, sometimes surprised innocence, rarely serenity. Despite the insistence of the Red Cross, the Russian military authorities have opened no investigation of the wells and graves replete with corpses. No court will judge the authors of such slaughter.

While we were at the Red Cross, a Chechen cameraman showed us a video of images of the bombing of Kadir Yurt on 28 March: twelve children were killed. The Russian High Command denied the attack occurred and blamed the disin-formation on a propagandistic maneuver by the "bandits."

Although the majority of the executions date back to March and April 1995, the roundups and arbitrary arrests continue.

At the *filter point* in the Staro-Promislovi district, depen-dent on the Russian Federation Ministry of the Interior in Chechnya, hundreds of detainees were interned at the begin-ning of June and each barracks is provided with dungeons for interrogation and torture. A youth called Salman related before the camera his journey and stay in one of them. In the truck that carried him, packed with dozens of suspects, the Russian soldiers killed eight of his companions who had protested against the conditions of their transportation and then drank vodka sitting on their corpses. The military com-mand issued a communiqué to the effect that the murdered were victims of bullets from independence guerrilla fighters.

The second protocol of the agreements signed on 10 June in Nazran stipulates the creation of a commission comprising six Russians and six Chechens to search out and identify those who have disappeared or been arrested in the seventeen months of war. Another clause agrees to the definitive closure of the *filter points*. But after so many broken promises and pacts, the Chechens awaited the results of the Russian elections without forging too many illusions as to Yeltsin's real intentions. Everything may continue as before and the desire for revenge on the part of the military commanders like Vladimir Shamanov and Viacheseav Tikomirov, humiliated by the failure of their brutal *pacification* and the disorganization and low morale of their troops, inevitably augurs nothing different. "The war," one of the leaders of the independence struggle later interviewed by me would say without boasting, "has lasted for two centuries. Who knows whether it will last another forty or fifty years?"

SHIFTING FRONTIERS

Unlike Bosnia, where the shortage of every kind of food and consumer good aggravated siege conditions, Chechnya still remains essentially well supplied. Along roads closely watched by the Russian army, and particularly in villages and at crossroads, diverse stalls and sales pitches stand in a line: drums of petrol, spare parts, used tires, refreshments, butchers, small tables of fruit and vegetables, and innumerable outlets for beer, vodka, and cigarettes. Such a plethora next to the control posts—fortified by sandbags and nests of machine guns—creates a deceptive impression of normality in the minds of visitors.

In Grozny's less ruined districts and streets, mudbound or flooded by the recent rains—the drainage system, like the water supply, no longer works—the spectacle is the same: the buying and selling of a wide range of articles, thanks to which unemployed, disoriented Chechens who have opted for passive resistance survive the harshness of the occupation.

The teeming Grozny market is like those in provincial cities of Anatolia and Iran: young money changers wave bundles of dollars; the crowd ebbs and flows between food and refreshment awnings, between stalls selling videos, radios, tapes, and tape recorders, argues over the stacks of cartons of American cigarettes, swirls round, and haggles over the prices of trousers, jackets, skirts, and blouses made in Turkey. My companion points out a packet of magdalenas from Spain! Everybody is carrying *Oakland* and *Men's Wear* plastic bags. The melée similarly attracts local criminals and informers for the puppet government. As we walk, I mentally note the profile of one bulldog-faced worthy dressed Mafia-style (or was it vice versa?) in a white, Al Caponesque floppy hat, whispering orders to his bank (or elsewhere) down his mobile phone.

Reality or a mirage?

This question hounds the visitor, lulled by the vista of the daily traffic and idyllic landscape of the supposedly "pacified" zones. The endless succession of control posts on the roads into Grozny guarantees, according to state television, a gradual normalization of life. On my travels through the different districts of Chechnya, I've met all manner of barriers and obstacles, around which civilian vehicles must maneuvre and zigzag: rebarbative blocks of cement, stones, metal posts, friezes, wire fences, beams, tree trunks, rusty caterpillar tank wheels. Papers are examined under a magnifying glass and car trunks are inspected at each halt. Does such a formidable display hermetically seal off the "safe zones" against Chechen fighters?

Nothing could be further from the truth. The Russian defense ministry pays its units several months in arrears and these frequently live on expedients, bribes, and pillaging. On the main thoroughfares, soldiers sell Chechens petrol from their tanks and, in more out-of-the-way areas, their guns, machine guns, weapons, and ammunition. The borders are permeable, changing: the military are afraid of nocturnal guerrilla attacks, do deals with neighboring villages, and lift barrier controls. That explains the ease with which independence fighters infiltrate "safe" cities like Gudermes and Sernovodsk, forcing the army to lay siege again and retake them with deluges of firepower, bringing enormous destruction. In Grozny itself, on 2 June a mine exploded under an armored car and four soldiers lost their lives. Six days later I heard the rat-a-tat-tat of machine-gun fire and violent mortar attacks as night fell: two more Russians died in twilight confrontation with the guerrilla or, according to other sources, from Chechen police bullets, downed by their official allies. Sometimes, it is members of a tank crew shooting into the air to terrify the population or make civilians cower, for no reason, except the effects of alcohol. During my stay I confirm several times that a few bottles of vodka are the best safe passes into the prohibited areas.

"The villages and settlements nominally controlled and evacuated by the army pass discreetly into the hands of the independence fighters," I'm told by Commander Ruslan Nasredtinov, one of the tenacious defenders of the town of

Goiskoye during its long, devastating siege. "Often, the Russians reasssert control and those accompanying them and restraining them are the independence fighters themselves, temporarily reintegrated into civilian life. When fighting stops in the areas deemed to be "pacified," our guerrilleros return home with their weapons and remain in a state of readiness till they receive orders to regroup and fight."

Our interview takes place in Kulari, the day after the *zikr* ceremony, which I attended through the mediation of Osman Imaiev, former public prosecutor of Chechnya and head of the delegation that signed the ceasefire agreements on 30 August 1995. Ruslan and his colleague Yacub—who has lost fifty relatives since the start of the war, seventeen of them "disappeared"—are two *murids* (members) of the *wird* (branch) of the *kadiri* brotherhood of Kunta Hadji: both in civilian dress, jeans and dark tunics, wearing the caps of the *tarika* (brotherhood) and trainers. Yacub, whose powerful black beard and passion in the execution of the Sufi ceremony held my attention, explains in turn the situation in "pacified" Chechnya while we share a table and food: that is, lumpy bread and sheep's cheese.

"The Russians look for a tacit agreement with the villages. For example, they have never stepped foot here. In fact, they coexist with an independence administration. There are four hundred communities in Chechnya. How many years would it take them to conquer and govern them all? Only if they notice a large concentration of guerrilleros, as is presently happening in Shali, do they besiege a town or city and proceed on a campaign of punishment to teach neighboring villages a lesson. They think that is the way to exterminate so-called "terrorists," but we cut through their lines at night and set up elsewhere.

"In Goiskoye they used artillery, helicopters, and airplanes; they fired illegal weapons. The civilian population fled and we fighters suffered more than a month's siege: from 4 April to 8 May last. Fortunately, many of the bombs did not explode and we recovered them and planted them as mines against their armored cars. They also suffered many losses."

The approximate number of Russian military casualties is much disputed and I ask him for his personal estimate.

"Nobody can give an exact figure, but the official figure of 2,500 should be multiplied at least five times. They usually bury their dead in common graves to avoid stirring up the population as happened during the war in Afghanistan. Others are transported to Russia in refrigerators or are devoured by dogs.

Ninety percent of the generals don't hide their Communist sympathies and thunder against Yeltsin. All the flags flapping over their bases and control posts sport the red of the USSR, not the colors of the Federation. We tease them like a *torero* with a bull: flick our capes and, whenever possible, stick in our *banderillas*. Those who had a bad time in Afghanistan, like General Bromov, oppose this war. They are animals who have learnt from experience and don't want to enter the bullring."

On Thursday, 6 June, I once again see the precarious nature of the Russian hold on the areas of the plain, officially under their control. After crossing a fenced-off zone, with pro-Russian government police, we venture into no-man's-land, set out with the inevitable stalls selling petrol and refreshments where the villagers while away their time.

When we reach Aleroi, a group of independence fighters escorts us to the base of Junkar Pasha Israpilov, commander of the southeast front who, along with Ruslan Gelayev, head of the southwest front, and Shamil Basayev, head of the central front, make up the Central command of Aslan Maschadov, leader of the Chechen Armed Forces and negotiator of the Nazran agreement of 10 June. Junkar Pasha is a youngish man, slim, fragile-looking, with well-balanced, expressive features. His left arm is bandaged and he invites us into a room with one of his aides: a green-eyed adult, possessed of that rough beauty, so common in Turkey, of some inhabitants of the Caucasus.

"I'm told you are the leader of the southeast front," I tell him. "We just came to see you and met no obstacles. What kind of front is this?"

There's a pause during which we are served tea.

"We have been ordered to break off all military action by President Yandarbiev whilst the peace discussions are in progress."

(He shows me the order.)

"But the Russians are still shooting," he adds. "Tonight their artillery bombed the village. The day before yesterday their air force attacked Baki Yurt and Gansolki, two villages in our territory. Daily they fly helicopters over, but our people don't react to these provocations nor to ones from mercenaries in the pay of Russia.

"Yeltsin uses every means of propaganda at his disposal to brand us as fanatics, fundamentalists, and bandits. This way, Europe can fold its arms and make the most of the profits offered by the breakup and auctioning of the USSR.

"We only ask for independence, the right to elect our own president and constitute a small, poor but free state. A state of citizens, regardless of their ethnic origins. I spent two years in Astrakhan, among Russians, and I would allow no persecution against them if they agree to live peacefully with us. But, if they continue the war, war they shall have. We will use all our weapons to defend ourselves. We will never accept their tutelage.

"They want to impose their culture and customs on us, they violate human rights at will. When we were children in the USSR, they inculcated in us hatred of Nazism and stiffened our resolve against it. But now we can see how Nazism has infiltrated the Russian Federation and its army. How else can one describe the state television newscaster who at peak time interviews two volunteers proudly displaying the severed ears of Chechen fighters?

"The war runs the risk of spreading to the rest of the Caucasus. If we cannot prosecute the struggle on our own, we will extend it elsewhere. We will not lay down our weapons until our land and liberty are restored.

"Say it loud and clear in your country. We are Muslims and that is why we have been struggling for two hundred years. All the soldiers under my command defend an ideal: to live freely, according to our traditions and laws."

The topic of conversation returns to the number of enemy losses.

"They try to deceive public opinion by hiding the real figures. In Shiri Yurt, in Shatoi district, there is a crematorium for incinerating corpses. They don't bury them, they burn them. Or send them in refrigerators to Rostov" (an article by the special correspondent of *Libération* confirms this [see *Les soldats inconnus de la guerre de Tchechenie,* 12 June 1996]). During the last lightning operation in Grozny, the official figure of eighty-nine dead disguised the real one: more than three hundred.

"The reinforcements are afraid and surrender without a fight. We have captured one of them three times and three times have let him go. Each time he cries and curses his leaders, but he doesn't have the courage to desert. On the other hand, we force no one to stay in our army: whoever wants to return to civilian life, can do so when he wishes."

Before bidding us farewell, Junkar Pasha Israpilov dictates to me a list of villages and settlements that have been razed—Stari-Achjoi, Orejovo, Goiskoye, all three in the district of Achjo-Martan; Serzhen Yurt, in the district of Shali; Zonaj, in Shatoi—and invites me to visit them, to see for myself the cruel and wanton devastation.

Goiskoye is a good example of the *scorched earth* policy, inherited from the Tsarist and Soviet regimes, aimed at subjugating the Chechens. Until a few months ago three hundred families lived in the village, that is, about fifteen hundred people. The seige begun on 4 April to capture a guerrillero unit—the one led by Rustan Nasredtirov and Yacub—lasted thirty-five days. The army used artillery, airpower, helicopters with Grad and Hurricane rocket-launchers, and fragmentation bombs. There are craters six meters wide and three meters deep: the mosque was toppled at one stroke. No houses are left standing: only walls, gutted buildings, strips of metal wiring, the leftovers from the conflagration. As I wander through the town, I make out the remains of stripped cars, mountains of debris, twisted cables, a burned-out tractor, a hat, a doorless refrigerator, a broken teapot, a manual of

Russian literature, remnants of carpets, door and window frames, scattered, rocket-blasted pieces of kitchen.

Ahmet Basiev, a older man with the appearance of a peasant, lives in the remains of what used to be his home, underneath an awning over bits of truncated furniture and carpets.

"This is my wealth," he says, forcing a smile. "Russia showed its power by destroying whole families, targetting women and children. Such barbarism deserves to be punished by a Genghis Khan."

As we talk, three helicopters fly over the area, vultures in search of carrion.

Weeds, shrubs, and flower-decked rose trees mercifully drape the scene of desolation.

TO THE MOUNTAINS

At the end of May, on the eve of the meeting between Yeltsin and the Chechen president Zelijman Yanarbiev, the army blocked all access to the town of Shali, some thirty kilometers from Grozny: the leadership had detected the presence of a large concentration of guerrilleros set on stimying pro-Russian Doku Zavgaiev's electoral farce. The response of the besieged was to lay siege to the barracks of the police and military command, paying back the occupying force in kind: siege for siege.

The tension mounted on 30 May with the assassination of the independence leader sent to negotiate, an outrage that frustrated the projected peace conversations in Daghestan, which were initiated days later in Ingushetia. On 2 June, the hard-line General Shamanov, right-hand man of the recently "resigned" Russian defense minister in Chechnya, demanded that the district elders surrender the rebels on pain of prolonging the siege and submitting the city to exemplary punishment. There was no surrender, no punishment, but the siege continued.

Shali was an area from which foreigners and journalists were banned.

On Thursday, 6 June, my attempt to reach there failed. After negotiating innumerable road controls with the help of magazines, lighters, and packets of cigarettes, we fell at the last hurdle: an officer inspected my papers and my companion's and we were ordered to turn back.

We repeated our attempt the following day: the officer on duty had changed and thanks to the efficient safe-conduct of a few bottles of vodka, he stamped our pass: the battered car in which we were traveling drove masterfully into no-man's-land, a strip of two or three kilometers where life was apparently being lived normally: stalls and sales pitches for petrol and refreshments were established at regular intervals on the road to Shali. On our entry into the city, we heard the dull thud of explosions, passed without problems through the independence fighters' control barrier, and emerged on an esplanade or main square dominated by a frenzy of activity that was incomprehensible at first sight.

Dozens of armed guerrilleros mounted guard on street corners or perched in windows or on roofs of neighboring buildings. Next to the mosque, a group of women and old men defiantly waved a framed photograph of Dudayev decorated with images of Imam Shamil and Kunta Hadji. Sorrowful cries go up of *allah akbar* (God is the greatest). We are in the place where on 18 January 1864, four thousand unarmed *murids*, disciples of Kunta Hadji, were victims of the firepower of the *blue uniforms* apostrophized by Lermontov: an evil act that left two hundred dead and a thousand wounded.

Almost a hundred and thirty years have gone by, but the situation remains identical, the protagonists the same. But what do Shamanov, Tichomirov, and the other *colonizers* from the Kremlin know of the sad "exploits" of their predecessors, noted by Baddely in *The Russian Conquest of the Caucasus?*

In spite of the cease-fire signed eleven days earlier, a helicopter has just bombed the Chechen security headquarters. The anger of the people packed into the square is the anger admirably described by Tolstoy. When they realize a foreign journalist—an outside witness—is there, he is surrounded by women and old men. Here is my transcription of their chorus of voices, as translated for me by Volodia, my companion and guide.

"Zavgaiev talked about coming here, but he'd better clear off to Russia. We don't want his illegal government! They've been killing us for the last two years. Why? Just because we want our Republic" (a woman in a headscarf).

"We demonstrate peacefully and they shoot us. The Russians say we're criminals. Look! There aren't any criminals or bandits here, just people asking for freedom" (an elderly woman).

"The Uzbeckis, Tayiki, Karahkstanis have their own countries. We are like them. We don't want to be Russian serfs. Freedom and independence!" (an older man, wearing a hat, carrying a shotgun).

"The Russians won't allow the press to come so the world doesn't know what's happening. Tell people we'd rather starve or freeze to death than accept slavery" (an old man who looks like a peasant).

There are bursts of machine-gun fire and we are ordered to disperse. My companion takes me to a pompous, colonnaded building, the Cultural Centre, now packed with guerrilleros. Soon Abu Movsaiev appears, security chief of the Chechen Republic of Ichkeria (that is how the Chechens describe their country), flanked by Aslanbel Ismailov, the man who orchestrated and participated in Shamil Basayev's daring incursion into Buddennovsk, in the heartland of Russia. Abu Movsaiev wears a track suit and bullet-proof jacket and carries a submachine gun over his shoulder. I notice two women fighters in his escort.

"Zavgaiev and his men wanted to call a 'council of ministers' here and couldn't," he explains. "That's why the Russians have taken retaliatory action. A few minutes ago they bombarded my headquarters and we returned fire.

"Our fighters are besieging the military command and police barracks. We won't attack: we want to negotiate the raising of the siege. But I think they're preparing a revenge attack."

Abu Movsaiev apologizes for the rushed exchanges and, for a few minutes, I walk round the square noting down the slogans which Volodia translates for me: "Long live Ichkeria! Death to the traitors!" insults directed at Yeltsin and the Russians.

On our return to Grozny along a deserted road—they allow no vehicles to pass and only women, the aged, and children to walk through—we cross army controls and stop at one flying the usual red flag adorned by an eye-catching image of Brezhnev. Volodia enters the sandbagged precinct, and thanks to the usual *safe-conduct* the soldiers welcome us with open arms.

They are volunteers, deceived by the official discourse about defending the endangered homeland and, according to which, those who fall on the field of honor, "do so with a smile on their lips" (thus spake Pavel Grachov). They live miserably. They show us a table protected from the sun by a makeshift awning: their daily food ration is reduced to a hunk of bread and lard, with a dash of pepper and salt: except for one Lebed suporter, the sympathies of the rest are split between Zyuganov and Zhirinovski. Vodka loosens their tongues and emotions: they like Spain and dream of the Canary Islands. One who is tall and thin, with a tooth missing, defends Zhirinovski and wants to know my opinion of him. I don't mince my words and mention his "original" proposal of a new division of Poland and his promise that "Russian soldiers will clean their boots on the beaches of the Indic Sea."

"Why not?" he replies. "Poland has always been a country divided between Germany and our Tsars. Without the traitors in power, we'd already be on the shores of India and in the Persian Gulf.

"Our commanders here are worthless. It's their fault we've lost more than ten thousand men. Can you imagine how many we'll lose if the war lasts ten years? Zhirinovski says: for every dead Russian, kill a hundred Chechens; for each ambush, raze a hundred villages to the ground. And, if they don't learn, we'll use nuclear weapons."

I mention the lessons of Vietnam, but he won't be persuaded. "The Americans aren't as tough as we are. Can you imagine them living in these conditions?"

We say good-bye, leave the checkpoint, and abandon them to half nostalgia, half wild-eyed stupor, beneath the flag with the resurrected countenance of Brezhnev. The explosive mixture of ultranationalism, frustrated imperial dreams, their hatred for the Chechens—who "should be destroyed like wild animals," as shown by those interviewed by the Duma deputy Nevzorov—illustrates the depths of confusion into which a great sector of the Russian population and intelligentsia, including Solzhenitsyn, has fallen. It is a breeding ground for salvation-bringing Messiahs, the identification of Stalin and Christ and the flourishing of Nazi groups like the "Russian Order," whose slogan, as communicated by its spokesman, Alexander Barkashov, is the "earliest possible elimination of Jews and gypsies."

The low morale of the army evident in Chechnya reveals the tensions existing between the commanders who support defenistrated Defense Minister Pavel Grachov and those who don't: the breach opened between a swaggering handful of generals and racist volunteers and the raw recruits, witnesses to the incompetence, barbarism and unlimited corruption of a war which they endure like a prison sentence, in conditions of penury, worthy of compassion.

If officers and petty officers are satisfied with vodka, as in the times of Nicholas, the appetites of their superiors, comfortably installed in Moscow, are much more voracious. "The newspaper *Izvestia*," wrote *El País* correspondent Pilar Bonet on 26 May 1996, "has revealed enormous losses in the Commercial Office of the Defence Ministry that, according to tax investigators, spent thousands of millions of roubles on the purchase of alcoholic drinks." According to the same correspondent, the man responsible for ministry finances, Vasili Vorovev, was sacked for "crass irregularities" while General Zherebtsov, architect of the most unpopular levy and others of his rank, have constructed "luxury *dachas* on the strength of the Defense Budget."

In these circumstances, it comes as no surprise that, as Alexander Lebed, the "new—for the moment—savior of the fatherland" stated, 30 percent of the soldiers were openly wondering "whether it wasn't time to point their guns in the other direction" and another 30 percent were thinking the same, but saying nothing. In the brittle atmosphere of an expiring reign and permanent conspiracy around Yeltsin, everything is possible: the Mafia and corrupt functionaries are ready to sacrifice whatever lives are necessary to preserve their fortunes and privileges, oblivious to the spectacle of the recruits in the high-risk, mountainous regions of Chechnya begging a crust of bread from passing vehicles.

On Sunday, 9 June, in torrential rain, we head south. My aim is to reach the fractious area of Vedeno and Bamut and interview the military leader of the sector, Shamil Basayev. But the blocked roads and unusable mudbound tracks prevent us getting beyond Shatoi, despite the skills of our driver.

After the first road controls and corresponding distribution of American cigarettes, the road winds down toward the broad, impetuous flow of the river Argun. A splendid panorama: the jagged mountains of the Caucasus push forward their wooded flanks veiled at intervals by strips of fog. In abrupt contrast with this natural beauty, the soldiers in the fortified stations and control posts dotting the route offer a picture of incredible poverty and dereliction: they stop the scant cars not to inspect the documentation of local villagers but to ask for spare cigarettes, bread, something to eat. They ask my companion whether anyone talks of demobilization; they are interested in the progress of the conversations with Aslan Maschadov, head of the Pro-Independence Command in Ingushetia. They all talk not of victory but of peace.

After we have crossed the bridge, we confront the remains of the mortar bomb ambush of 16 April: more and more burned-out tanks, rusty artillery pieces scattered over the hillside, a small cross planted by the soldiers in a silent but eloquent protest against the futility of their immolation. The road is a succession of control posts, damp, down-at-heel encampments, nests of machine guns manned by youths numb with cold, vistas of poorly clothed, underfed recruits, warming their hands around miserable fires. From time to time, we have to stop and give way to a long column of T90 combat vehicles, each serviced by a tank crew of a dozen.

The rain is relentless and soaks the ferns and the climbing plants prospering like roadside waterlilies. They are the landscapes wonderfully described by Lermontov and Tolstoy: slopes clothed in firs, scarps, mists, a strange watchtower that probably acted as a lookout point for the *murids* of Mansur and Shamil. The evidence of the *scorched earth* policy is also the same: burned houses near Zonaj and buildings destroyed, draped in sadness and rancor.

Shatoi is equally desolate: in its central market, constructed by the tsars, half a dozen stalls still survive against a back-cloth of ruins. The central square, the town hall, were fodder for the flames. A slogan in Arabic characters cries out in desperation: *allah akbar.*

Three days of uninterrupted rain, waterlogged land, mud-flats, rivers that have spilled over their banks, and stretches blocked by debris force me to abandon my plans. We drive back to Grozny.

My indignation at the devastation and atrocities inflicted by the occupying forces merge at the end of my stay with feelings of anxiety and sorrow at the fate of Russia. The executioners are, after all, the victims of broken dreams and utopias, of ancestral resignation to the arbitrary ways of their despots and Messiahs.

As the film director Andrei Konshalkovski wrote recently, "The Orthodox mentality shapes a collective consciousness. People don't feel individually responsible for their acts. They always find someone else to be responsible: God, the Government, the Tsar, Stalin, Brezhnev. Nobody wants to admit that anything is their fault?"

Will Russians one day accept their overwhelming responsibility for the brutal crushing of Chechnya?

APPROACHES TO ISLAM

1

Midway through the fifteenth century, as the predictable outcome of the Reconquest of Islamic Spain offset the fall of
Byzantium and devastating Ottoman advances, Juan de
Segovia, a Spanish bishop whose previous claim to fame had
been his opposition to the dogma of papal infallibility at the
Council of Constance, put before the hierarchy in Rome an
original and revolutionary proposal as to the relationship
between Christianity and Islam. It was on the eve of a fresh
outbreak of military, political, and religious conflict, when
mutual ignorance in both camps and the suppression of reality by highly negative, stereotypical images were stoking
expectations of an inevitable clash of civilizations. Yet Juan
de Segovia commissioned an Islamic scholar to translate the
Koran with the laudable aim of *audi alteram partem*—listen-
ing to the other side—and then argued it would be oppor-
tune to call a council of the two religions to lay a foundation
for a possible future peace throughout the world.

The Spanish bishop, whose role and ideas have been
analysed by Robert Southern, suggested a three-stage *rap-
prochement* of the rival contenders: a truce, the length of
which should be negotiated, when all armed engagements
would be halted; an intervening period when diplomatic,
commercial, and cultural relations would be established to
improve understanding on each side; and, once a climate of
trust and conciliation had been developed, an assembly of
religious authorities should be held, which would work to
determine the common ground existing between both parties, rather than to emphasize the differences of dogma that
separated them. Unlike Ramón Lull and the writers going
back to Abélard, Juan de Segovia, though convinced of the
superiority of his beliefs, did not preach the conversion of
Muslims. The latter were susceptible to the influence of persuasion and example, not to the methods, however peaceful,
of a crusading spirit. As we know, the idea of such a council

was duly rejected and its author shut up in a Swiss monastery where he perished unheralded and forgotten.

Over the last fifteen years I have often recalled the truncated endeavors of this unusual Spaniard whose historical vision has unfortunately maintained a vital relevance undimmed by the centuries that have gone by. The Iranian revolution—which the West failed to predict and whose aftermath it incorrectly analysed—the resistance and subsequent radicalization of Afghan *mujaheddin*, the terrorism of Palestinian extremists, or Gaddafi's braggadocio have meanwhile revived an atmosphere of confrontation which, we should remember, is consubstantial with the very idea of Europe. Eclipsed for a time by the imminent Soviet threat, the representation of Islam as the ineluctable enemy on the doorstep has gradually been recovering its old immediacy. The collapse of communism and formidable military incursions in the Gulf have rapidly transformed the new world order trumpeted by George Bush into the minefield we tread today. A strange *New World Symphony*, with slight thematic variations led by different conductors, resounding in our ears from Bosnia, Somalia, and Rwanda to the greater glory of the architects of this miraculous peace! The gradual growth of Islamism from Malaysia to the Maghreb means that prophets of the new cold war like Samuel Huntington are already announcing the inevitable *clash of civilizations* that will structure the twenty-first century: a lethal struggle pitting Islamists —identified with terrorism, intolerance, the violation of human rights, and all manner of obscurantism—against the democratic, liberal, capitalist lay world of the West. Huntington's arguments depend on massive recourse to the clichés and anathemas the two bands routinely throw at each other: the image of a corrupt and corrupting West, arrogantly defending new forms of colonialism and imbued with an unrelenting hatred of Islam, as portrayed by some political and religious leaders from within the vast, complex, contradictory Muslim universe; and the image of a violent, homogeneous, fanatical Islam whose raison d'être is its hostility to the West. Anyone with any knowledge of the two civilizations will recognise how such schematic appraisals turn extremes into norms. Nobody, I believe, would ever dream of portraying IRA terrorists or Karadžić's *chetniks* as spokesmen for the West or for Christianity; but the news media in Europe and North America, supported by a few intellectuals and futurologists, draw general conclusions from scraps of evidence and mistake the Armed Islamic Group in Algeria and the most radical theocracies for Islam as a whole.

Consequently, a climate has been created of ideological, political, and cultural confrontation that is very similar to the one that obtained in other historical periods but which displays very different characteristics. To start with, it has to be said that Huntington's theses run the risk of encouraging Western and Islamic ultras in their xenophobic campaigns: Karadžić's Serbs, self-styled saviors of Europe, by dint of their *ethnical cleansing* from the threat of an "Islamic Caliphate" in the Balkans; a Greek Orthodox Church absorbed in the severe spirit of the Crusade; Islamists erradicating the ancient Coptic Church from Egypt; inspirers and executors of *fatwas* against foreigners and "infidels" in the bloody chaos that is Algeria. Adoption of such logic would reintroduce into our mental schema the notion of a *fifth column:* both the twelve million Muslims established in Europe and the millennary Christian minorities in the Middle East would become hostages and scapegoats in a global confrontation reviving the specters of expulsions, massacres, and exodus. After all, aren't the Serb radicals already using the language of the old Christians of Spain by labeling as Turks the newly threatened Muslim minority in Europe, the new *moriscos?*

I do not think it at all idle to set the perspective of Juan de Segovia against that of Huntington and his ilk. A Spanish point of view, based on the rich lessons from our historical experience, in relation to the conflict of civilizations apparently looming over the horizon can perhaps shed some light on aspects both of the problem and the positions that are being adopted. The somewhat symmetrical destinies of Spanish and Islamic civilizations invite such an approach. The Islamism propagated at an individual level throughout the Muslim world merits examination from a perspective beyond that of those who, right or wrong, feel worried and alarmed by the phenomenon. The primary duty of intellectuals is to try to make it *understandable* without necessarily implying *rendering it acceptable*.

In the debate I am proposing, I intend to put forward hypotheses, not theses. The historical parallels are enriching, illuminate and connect dark areas and disparate events, but cannot be taken as the only point of reference. Each society, each epoch contains particular characteristics that cannot be assimilated to previous civilizations and periods.

Arguments must be advanced tentatively, without any attempt to lay down the law. The ideas sketched here need to be aired in discussion: they are interim, problematic, malleable, and only aspire to invigorate a debate, free from any corpus of dogma or instruments of ideological pressure.

2

The first new element in this crucial stage of relations between the West and Islam is the emergence of voices from within the Islamic world which argue that conflict with the Islamists is inevitable and speak out in defense of the ideas and values of the Western world: as happened fifteen years ago in Iran, intellectuals, secular parties and associations, political movements, and feminist groups in Algeria, Egypt, and the Indian subcontinent are emerging as the front-line troops in such a confrontation. Unable to solve the problems faced by their societies, discredited in the eyes of their peoples by authoritarianism, arbitrary behavior, and corruption, the nationalist and socialist regimes—in reality under a military thumb—have been a fiasco nurturing, parallel to the great expansion of Islamism, the creation of Westernized elites who accommodated to these regimes for good or bad and now confront the dilemma of defending them or enduring a model of society that directly clashes with the political and cultural values they have adopted from the West.

The conflict, in its present phase, is less between the West and Islam—however much the reality of an arrogant, domineering West, alert only to its neocolonial interests, is demonized, as I mentioned, by some governments and armed Islamic movements—than between Islamists and non-Islamists, traditionalists and reformers, the religious and the secular *within Islam itself.* A clash that assumes very different guises, as the disparate examples of Iran, Algeria, the Sudan, or Saudi Arabia bear witness.

The penetration of ideas developed during the Enlightenment and the French Revolution into most of the Islamic world, though often superficial—Turkey constitutes a case apart—created Europeanized minorities who support them and now stand in the firing line of a mass movement that Europeans consider retrograde and fanatical.

Thus, it is not the old political and military struggle of one block against another—as was the case between the eighth and seventeenth centuries—but, as a consequence of Europe's global triumph and its past colonial hold over Muslim peoples, it is a struggle between Western values and ways of life judged by some to be desirable and valid and by others to be contaminating and hostile. In other words, no one can deny the European origin of the ideas and models whose pros and cons are being debated, and the confrontations they provoke primarily concern Muslims though there may be repercussions in the West (terrorism, xenophobia, the harrassing and subsequent radicalization of immigrants poorly integrated in their new countries).

I have more than once drawn a parallel between the decadence of Arab culture from the fourteenth century and Spanish decadence, which came three centuries later. After several hundred years of splendor, when they enlightened the known world of the day and eagerly assimilated Western, Eastern, Indian, and Mediterranean learning, both faded and entered a period of hibernation. The great thinkers, scientists, poets, and mystics of Islam were fought and their manuscripts condemned to burn or gather dust by the *ulema* and scholars (as they are to this day by the Wahhabis who lord it over Mecca): the vigor of Arab civilization declined and was transformed into a barren waste. Ibn Khaldun's melancholy before the decline of Islamic society anticipates that of Cervantes with respect to Spain. The ruins of both societies weigh heavily on the desolate horizons of their present.

When Ferdinand and Isabel and their heirs abolished the fertile medieval coexistence of the three Hispanic castes and enforced an intransigent homogeneity, Spanish culture gradually succumbed to the asphyxiating atmosphere. The cordon sanitaire Philip II imposed on his kingdoms, described by the French scholar Marcel Bataillon, completed his great-grandparents' cleansing operation and led to the eradication of all that was different: an "energetic reaction by the nation" (thus spake nineteenth-century neo-Catholic polymath Menéndez Pelayo) finished off Erasmists, Lutherans, and quietists in a matter of decades. Spanish Muslims, the *moriscos*, were forced to convert and live a clandestine Islam and the Holy Office systematically pursued the converted and their descendants until it was abolished by Joseph Bonaparte. The consequences of that autistic self-absorption and inquisitorial vigilance over possible "germ carriers" created a framework very similar to the totalitarian systems of the twentieth century: ideological and national orthodoxy, self-sufficiency, a repudiation of the alien, hostility to any modernizing project, a retreat into petrified values, an obsessive fear of being infected by the "enemy."

The decadence of Arab and Spanish culture, though experienced in different contexts, was in both cases the result of internal causes. External events—Tamerlaine's Mongol invasion, whose effects Hichem Djait has analysed so pertinently, the exhausting military and economic effects occasioned by the struggle against the Protestant Reformation, and so forth were clearly contributing factors. But in both cases the results were identical: they uncoupled Spain and the Arab world from the train of progress and modernity.

Before analysing the impact of this historic backwardness and the ways proposed to cut it short, I will touch on a subject marginal to the central thread of this essay, but that may nevertheless help put it in context: the surprising parallel that exists between sixteenth-century Spain and the contemporary Saudi monarchy or the Kuwaiti emirate.

Thanks to Américo Castro, Domínguez Ortiz, Caro Baroja, Márquez Villanueva, and other historians we now have a fund of reliable information about the social structure of Habsburg Spain, a state in which the medieval system of the separation of the castes survived in latent form despite the decree expelling the Jews and the abolition of the statute allowing Muslims to stay: at the top of the hierarchy, old Castilians, fortified by hidalgo pride and "blood untainted by any bad stock or impurity," contemptuous of artesan trades and branches of knowledge branded as Jewish and gazing favorably only on the military and the clergy, the church and the army; in the middle, converted Jews, charged with the technical, economic, and intellectual duties of their ancestors (one only has to recall Cervantes who, after being wounded in Lepanto and imprisoned in Algiers, was unable to emigrate to America—a privilege reserved for old Christians—and received as a reward for his pains the humble, vilified post of tax collector); and at the bottom, the *moriscos*, condemned to the lowliest jobs and to providing cheap labor for the large estates of the nobility.

As Sir Richard Burton perceptively noted in his work dedicated to the *hadj* or Muslim pilgrimage to Mecca, the caste pride of the Bedouins, already partly adepts of Wahhabi doctrine, their aversion to manual trades and work in general irresistibly bring to mind the attitudes of old Castilians. This attitude to life and consequent division of labor still structures Saudi society. The noble tribes, with their retainers and relatives, comprise the highest caste, which governs in an absolutist and theocratic vein; intellectual, economic, and technical affairs are largely managed by foreigners—Palestinians, Egyptians, Lebanese—though in the fields of banking and finance they are now being replaced by Western-educated Saudis; the humble lot of the *morisco* falls to immigrants from Islamic countries: Pakistanis, Bangladeshis, Malayans, Filipinos. They are laborers, oil-field workers, road builders, or domestic servants to princes and aristocrats grown fabulously rich on black gold. Like sixteenth-century Castilians, the Saudis and Kuwaitis are not above the sumptuous lifestyles or advances in technology that come from the outside world: they enjoy them while outlawing the climate of freedom that led to their creation as contrary to their own religious principles and social norms. In contemporary Kuwait and Saudi Arabia—invaded by Western and Japanese technology—luxury cars, air conditioning, mobile phones, and the whole range of computers are common currency, but their subjects have no access to Western books that are judged to be harmful or, and still worse, to the remarkable heritage of Arab culture, be it rationalist, poetic, historical, or mystical.

Just as the Spanish clung to their nationalist-religious dogmas, prided themselves on their ignorance, and poured the wealth from the gold of the Americas into the building of palaces and churches rather than investing in commodity production and the expansion of trade—thus encouraging the transfer of money to the vaults of their creditors, the bankers in The Hague and Amsterdam—the huge income from the black gold born in the Arabian desert, after satisfying the plentiful needs of princes and aristocrats and the more modest ones of the rest of their compatriots, also finds its way to the big banks and financial institutions of London and New York where it is recycled on the economic helter-skelter of Western capitalism.

When Sadam Hussein took possession of Kuwait, only 10 percent of the holdings of the National Bank were in the emirate!

As the example of Spain shows, sudden wealth unearned by one's own effort does not change the mentality of the beneficiaries. Spanish nobles and hidalgos, hostile to science and culture, simply deferred to the dogmas of a church that was opposed to the innovations driven by the Reformation, which centuries later would lead to capitalism and the *Encyclopédie*, the French Revolution and industrialization: "An economy is above all," writes Américo Castro, "the result of the attitude a people adopts with respect to itself, the world around them and the divine forces under whose rule they think they exist." Miguel de Unamuno's famous 'Let them invent!' belatedly echoes an attitude that at the turn of the century was finally being challenged by the real driving forces in Spanish society, but that to this day remains dominant in the petro-dollar monarchies of the Arabian peninsula.

Will the chimera of gold which was so decisive in Spain's economic ruination one day be followed by the phantom of black gold and all manner of unpredictable repercussions on a compact if fragile Saudi society? Unlike the precedent from Spanish history, oil has enriched and transformed the material life of the inhabitants of the Saudi kingdom; but can the present "caste" system survive a destructive clash with modernity and the internal Islamist radicalization that is silently being forged?

3

The key word put about to define the position of the Arab elites, particularly after the Gulf War, is humiliation. Humiliation in relation to the power of the West and its policy of double standards vis-à vis Kuwait and Palestine, the humiliation of their colonial past and the corrupt despotism of the governments that have come with independence, humiliation arising from struggles and clan rivalries that are the very opposite of the ideal of the *Umma;* humiliation before the crushing military, economic, technological, political, and cultural superiority of the West, a feeling exposed in public and private with a mixture of grief and impotence, fruit of a sense of backwardness that is difficult to overcome and of the threat hanging over them: the mass of humanity taking to the streets to protest against their exclusion from society in the name of Islamic religious principles. In the complicated situation they find themselves in, many writers and intellectuals based in Europe or with a predominantly European education tend to cast off the entire Arab tradition as if it were a dead weight despite the rich splendors of its past, and they fail to detect there the presence of the seeds of modernity, of what still retains life after so many centuries.

The Spanish are very familiar with such sentiments and gut reactions, having experienced them in our own flesh. As Marcel Bataillon showed in his day, the potential growth of peninsular intellectual and economic life was thwarted in the mid–sixteenth century. The thesis that a Spain unified by Ferdinand and Isabel would have been a nation like other European nations conceals a pious deceit aimed at stanching wounded pride. Old Christian attitudes to trade, industry, work, and, in general, to the economy set Hispanic Man apart from Modern Economic Man. In the reign of Charles II, Spain was like a sleeping beauty or enchanted kingdom, outside the developments of history. In the middle of the eighteenth century, at the height of the Enlightenment, universities still taught the scholasticism of St. Thomas Aquinas, discussed whether an angel could go in a single flight from Lisbon to Madrid, and dubbed Aristotelian physics "Old Christian" in opposition to the "ultra-Jewish" physics of Galileo. In consequence, nineteenth-century Spain constituted a "human community devoid of science and needing outside help in the most trivial matters" (Américo Castro).

The writings of travelers to the peninsula from the second half of the seventeenth century describe a world whose ideals, beliefs, standard of living, and customs are light-years behind those of other Europeans. They all express their horror at the Inquisition's *autos-da-fé*, attended by a general public in festive spirit. Whether we Spaniards like it or not, the phrase *l'Afrique commence aux Pyrénees* relates to an objective reality. Alongside the patronizing eulogies of the exotic or picturesque in Spanish life, the condemnation of fanaticism and backwardness was beyond dispute. A typical visitor, like the famous Casanova, encouraged the Spanish in incendiary prose to break their chains and abandon their lethargy, to embark upon a complete revolution of their institutions and lives, to end once and for all their holidays from history. His well-intentioned rhetoric anticipates, as we shall see, the one now directed by the spokesmen for European modernity at Arab countries, "sunk in a sea of religious fanaticism, despotism and superstition."

The reaction of enlightened Spanards in many ways evokes that of Arab intellectuals of the *Nahda* (Renaissance) a century later. In the peninsula the critiques of foreigners were felt to be both a reflection of a harrowing reality and an unbearable source of shame: it was necessary to get rid of the dross of history, take on the doctrines of progress, and be as European as everyone else. France was the model to be imitated and enlightened Spanish intellectuals soaked up its language, customs, political and philosophical ideas, and agnosticism. But, although influential at the court of Charles III, they comprised a tiny minority and were soon to be nicknamed the *afrancesados.* Bonaparte's invasion and the popular uprising against reforms that were necessary but imposed from outside by force of arms, provoked a cruel split in their ranks. Some embraced the cause of the invaders, were judged to be traitors and fled with the French. Others made common cause with the people, realizing their liberal and constitutional aims were out of step with the beliefs of "deepest" Spain. The majority to which they now adhered from a sense of patriotism demanded a return to the hated past of religious, monarchist absolutism.

The defeat of the *afrancesados*—who, *toutes proportions gardées*, so remind me of the spokesmen for the *hizb faransa* or "French Party" denounced in Algeria by the Islamists—led to a return to an inward-looking, narrow-minded Spain although the seeds they had sown and the spirit of the times did lead to a resurgence of their ideas: the country was divided between traditionalists and liberals, a division ever-present in the civil wars that bloodied the peninsula throughout the last century. All in all, reactionary Catholic nationalism won out on almost every occasion— after ephemeral Republican experiences in 1873 and 1931, and longer periods of shared power (1875–1923)—culminating in Franco's crushing victory in 1939.

Eighteenth- and nineteenth-century Spain thus provides numerous points of comparison with Muslim countries re-created or established after the colonial experience (Turkey forged by Ataturk is a case apart and should be studied as such): backwardness, arbitrariness habits, despotism, dependence on European science and technology, lack of creative freedom, a weak or nonexistent middle class, and a dominant traditional style of religiosity. Viewed with suspicion over the centuries, reforming ideas arrived as imports from abroad and were labeled as alien and undermining. The motley crew comprising the "Anti-Spain" (liberals, democrats, republicans, masons, anarchists, socialists, communists) could never escape that insulting tag. Blanco White's memorable pages on the attempts by Seville's clergy in the late eighteenth century to regulate the clothes worn by women brings to mind those of francophone North African novelists on the subject of the veil and the *hjab*.

Although Spain did not suffer colonial or semicolonial dependency like almost all of the Muslim countries and incongruously even allied itself to the "civilizing African mission" of the European powers, the backwardness of its society and the Europeanizing endeavors of its elites brought in their train almost identical consequences.

Rejection of obscurantist Spain incarnated by Franco and compensatory admiration of anything foreign led me, for example, to replace Catholic nationalist *indoctrination* with a *countereducation* that jettisoned en bloc the values of the past. I needed later *training* to rid myself of my prejudices and finally grasp the importance and modernity of the Spanish heritage, despite the way it had been brutally savaged over the centuries.

The intellectual life and customs of the Europeanized elites in Muslim countries is shaped by the same propensity to devalue their own tradition (the Arab-Islamic legacy) and slavishly imitate whatever comes from abroad (the culture and values of the West); it is the reverse side of the coin of their humiliation and superficial anticolonialist rhetoric. If scientific and technological backwardness has forced Spaniards and Arabs to import their knowledge from the generating centers in Europe and North America, Spain's more or less successful adaptation to modernity and its values to which I shall refer later has not entirely erased its reticence and complexes with respect to an uncomfortable past.

But we should return to our central thread. The reforming impulse in two cultures that are as ancient and rich, as structured and complex as the Spanish and Arab, despite the decadence they suffered or are suffering, cannot come from outside unless elements exist within the religious nucleus of their own cultural identity ready to generate their own transformation. What has happened in Spain over the last thirty years is an eloquent example of that, but it remains to be seen whether similar elements and internal mechanisms are present and will some day act within the nerve-center of Islam.

4

The origins of the Protestant Reformation can be traced back
to a profound social and religious reaction against the abandoning of the Christian principles of the Gospels by the
papacy and the highest echelons of the Church hierarchy.
Luther's horror at the depravations of the Church in Rome
was immediately echoed by the common people as much as
by artesans, traders, and the scholars who frequented universities and centers of learning. His passionate discourse
was aimed at the princes of the Church and their allies, the
monarchs and nobles. Protestant doctrine rapidly spread
through Germany and northern countries, and soon split into
various factions: some sought compromises with local poten-
tates in exchange for the formal conversion of a king, prince,
or burgomeister, where others postulated a violent, radical
type of Christian communism. Religious wars laid Europe
waste for almost two centuries: Spain, the states of the Italian
peninsula, and, after dissension and internal strife, France,
remained faithful to the authority of the pope; the Low
Countries, England, Scandinavia, and most of Germany
embraced diverse currents of Lutheranism, Calvinism,
Anglicanism, and so on of the Reformation movement.
Outbreaks of the new doctrine were mercilessly crushed in
Spain and the influential and active French Protestants were
persecuted and massacred until they went into exile or were
expelled. Within the camp of the reformed Church, quarrels
over doctrine led to tens of thousands of deaths. The tidal
wave of renewal that swept through Europe, whether it was
victorious or defeated, changed the course of Christianity: it
was a social and individual phenomenon, it affected equally
political and religious institutions, the intimate lives of people, and their behavior and consciences. The wars, crimes,
and clashes that bloodied the Old World were countered by
new models of political coexistence and a change in the
behavior of the individual within the framework of society.

The Puritans who set sail in the *Mayflower* pursued the fulfilment of a religious and earthly ideal. Calvinism, as many historians have demonstrated, laid the bases for capitalist development and democracy imbued with Christian principles and had no more than a tangential, incidental impact on Islam, then headed by the Ottoman conqueror.

The Muslim world is today at the beginning of the fifteenth century of the Hegira, that is, a century before Luther's confrontation with the Bull of Indulgences and the Ausburg Confession drawn up by Melanchton. Like the Christianity of that period, it is being swept by a powerful movement for inner renewal after the collapse of the hopes placed on imported socialism (Nasserism, the FLN, Baathism in Syria, Iraq, and so forth): it is driven by an individual, ethical, religious impulse that aspires to transform the whole of society. The Islamist creed—like the Protestant one—displays a variety of disparate characteristics and forms: it is radically anti-Western in Iran, as a result of North American support for the regime of the shah and the aggression of Sadam Hussein; violent and merciless in Algeria, where the Armed Islamic Group (GIA) has abandoned the principles of Sunni orthodoxy with respect to the shedding of the blood of Muslims and the "unfaithful" to adopt in practice the extremist doctrine of the *kharijis* who ruled over Algeria in the ninth and tenth centuries of the Christian calendar; it is flexible and able to integrate itself in the parliamentary system in Jordan, Bangladesh, and indirectly in Morocco through the opposition's electoral program. In turn, some political groups in the Near East who support anti-Israeli and anti-Western terrorism claim to belong to the movement. The lay regimes of Iraq, Syria, Tunisia, and Egypt endure and repress Islamist incursions with an iron hand or try to negotiate a compromise. What the Western press describes as *the black tide of Islam* extends from the Pacific to the Atlantic and affects not only governments and institutions but tens of millions of people in the realm of their individual consciences.

The first movement to re-Islamize Muslim society, with the intention of purifying it of all superstition and surface accretions goes back to the eighteenth century and was the work of the Wahhabis. Their founder, Mohammed Abdul Waheb, was a distant disciple of a fourteenth-century treatise writer, Ibn Taymiya, known for his attacks on the esoteric views of Ibn Arabi. His preaching won over the Bedouin tribes of the Hiyaz, whose primitive, spartan conditions of life readily adapted to severe religiosity, quite removed from the compromises and accommodations of the Muslim societies of Egypt, Palestine, Syria, and Mesopotamia.

The traveler from Barcelona, Domingo Badía, better known by his pseudonym of Ali Bey, has left us an animated description, together with a lucid commentary, of the first Wahhabi forays in the Arabian peninsula. Their religious and social ideas, he predicted, would face serious obstacles to further extension into richer, more advanced regions because of their rigid norms. "If they don't somewhat relax the harshness of their principles, I think it impossible for Wahhabism to spread to other countries beyond the desert."

Ali Bey was right, but he could not foresee the discovery of oil that followed the conquest of Arabia by Abdul Waheb's disciples. If the doctrine of the Saudis has some points of contact with the early Lutheran Reformation and its project of re-Christianizing—in this case re-Islamizing—society, in practice it lacks the former's socially revolutionary vision and defense of the free interpretation of the sacred texts that opened the door to freedom of conscience and the birth of modern capitalism. The tribal hierarchy of the Bedouins, with its clear division of roles and labor, anchors the first Islamist state in a social immobility similar to that of Habsburg Spain. Despite the enormous economic power with which it finances numerous religious movements and holy works and its control of the holy places of Islam, Wahhabism has not managed to spread beyond the frontiers of its kingdom. The reforming Salafi drive failed in Morocco and the Muslim brothers, brutally fought by Nasser, did not succeed in imposing their rule in Egypt. Today, a newly minted Islamism, with different policies in Iran, the Sudan, and Algeria, combines various shades and degrees of religious severity with a social message aimed at the huge mass of marginalized Muslims excluded—even deprived of their marks of identity—by the regimes spawned by decolonization. Saudi theocracy holds no attractions for present-day Islamic societies: its tarnished role in the Gulf War and absolute dependency on the North American protector have irremediably burnt its bridges with those who, from Indonesia to the Maghreb, seek to unite the social and the religious in a vision of society that is still diffuse but which is aimed both against governments labeled as illegitimate and despotic and also against "the oil-rich hoarders," the "abusive beneficiaries" of the pilgrimage and *Beit el Haram.*

5

Writers like Bernard Lewis have described the long, tortuous
process of the adaptation to Islamic climes of concepts like
secularism, parliamentarianism, republicanism, democracy,
and so on. With the exception of Turkey, these concepts
were introduced by colonizers—sometimes in the guise of a
protectorate or mandate—who may have spread the news
but refrained from putting them into practice. Such defects at
source throw light on the reservations and suspicion with
which they were welcomed by the colonized masses.
Nevertheless, they sowed the seed in the urban elites and
quite unintentionally encouraged the independence movements in Asia and Africa. In this way the anti-imperialist
struggle handed these Europeanized nationalists a unitary
platform around which to rally their peoples. But once independence had been gained either through negotiated deals
or war, the new regimes in Muslim countries, usually led by
the military, applied their European political recipes in a
clumsy, self-interested way that had the predictable outcome
of discrediting them forever in the eyes of the masses. The
nationalist socialism of charismatic leaders like Nasser and
Boumedien, like the crudest pragmatism of their successors,
led to the cultural and social marginalization of a majority of
the people and a disenchanted perception of their regimes as
alien to Islamic tradition and society, in spite of the pirouettes
of some leaders searching for the roots of Marxism in the
surah of the Koran.

The reaction to Arab "humiliation" and the failures of the
nationalist and secular governments could only come from the
religious quarter. Neither the demonization of the West by
Khomeini nor the horrors of the civil war in Algeria should
keep us from recognising one essential fact: Islamism confers
on the huge mass excluded from the benefits of the new ecumenical dogma of the West—ultraliberalism, monetarism,
untrammeled trade, the planet conceived as a Global Shopping

Mall—a consciousness to identify with and a model of behavior to imitate in the framework of their societies which, although in many respects quite shocking—the *actual* status of women, for example—may constitute a dynamic, motivating factor in the necessary restructuring of these societies. For some Arab peoples, an Islamist system distanced from the "Caliphate" of the GIA and the terrorism of fanatical groups would, *in the present phase*, probably be more tolerable than the oppressive regimes which now govern them.

Hassan el Tourabi, the spiritual leader of the Sudanese military junta and one of the most outstanding representatives of the Islamist tendency, sets out ideas in an article (*Liberation*, 8 May 1994) that, although belied by the Sudanese regime's brutal sectarian policies, do at least merit analysis and discussion:

> neither nationalism nor socialism succeeded in mobilising our societiethe path of development . . . while religion may be the most powerful engine for development. . . . These words may perhaps sound strange to the ears of a rich Westerner. But, what was the role of Puritanism in America when civilising that savage land was on the agenda? What was the role of the Protestant ethic in the take-off of the European economies? Religion is a factor in development!

The concrete reference to Protestantism and the ideals it embodied at its inception can at least help us to replace the present schema of a clash of civilizations proposed by politicians (Charles Pasqua) and intellectuals (Huntington) with stubborn, enduring realities and to situate it in a historic perspective that is both less frenzied and more fruitful.

I spoke earlier of Spain and of the obstacles encountered by reforming ideas—those of Protestants, the Enlightenment, liberals, republicans, socialists—considered alien by a good number of people and furiously opposed by nationalist Catholicism up to Franco's victorious Crusade. It is only superficially paradoxical that it was precisely in the years of Francoist dictatorship, enforced by fire and sword to demolish a "Jewish-Masonic-Atheist" Republic, that the seeds of change sprouted that would allow Spain to emerge from centuries of backwardness and cast off the straitjacket constraining it. If the Opus Dei technocrats deserve any recognition it must be for the way they successfully removed guilt from the confused attitude of Spanish Catholicism to the profitable use of money and nurtured in the country the Calvinist ethic of *the pursuit of wealth leads to God.*

What neither the Protestant Reformation nor any of the political and cultural movements of later centuries achieved, despite the relentless efforts of Europeanized secular and democratic elites, was introduced by a team of politicians and economists that emerged with disconcerting ease from the hard core of Hispanic Catholicism. Spanish ways of thinking changed radically in less than a decade (tourism and working-class emigration to Europe also played their part). The bourgeoisie was strengthened and acquired a modern coloration. The economic takeoff rendered the system designed by Franco anachronistic, and it collapsed like a house of cards upon the death of the Caudillo: Spain was definitively modern and young socialist leaders reaped the fruits of seeds sown by their Opus Dei predecessors. For once, the impetus had come from within.

Might a similar phenomenon take place in the world of Islam? The hypothesis should not be dismissed out of hand even though it can't be tested at the moment. The social composition and cultural atmosphere in Muslim countries is obviously different from that in Spain. There is as yet no middle class that can be compared to the Spanish bourgeoisie of thirty years ago nor will the world economic conjuncture allow a rerun of the decade of expansion of the 1960s: the future of developing countries is today compromised by the new international order so lucidly analysed by Ricardo Petrella: "One essential point remains to be resolved: the free personal interpretation of the *koran* similar to that which encouraged individual initiative and freedom of conscience among Protestants. Without that, any possible parallel with Lutheran of Calvinist doctrine loses credibility and becomes merely a propaganda weapon." At any rate, a parallel between Spain and the multiple diversity of the Muslim world affords an opportunity to examine Islamism from other less partisan, less circumstantial perspectives. An evocation of the horrors, suffering, and massacres occasioned by the religious wars of Europe does not authorize one to excuse those currently devastating some Islamic countries, but it may help one to understand better the undeniable reality of the re-Islamizing of Muslim society from Tangiers to Jakarta without that excluding, as I pointed out at the beginning, outright condemnation of the terrorist methods used by the GIA and other extremist groups, that go against all the principles and laws of Islam. An ecumenical vision, like that of Juan de Segovia, is undoubtedly more necessary than ever. Neither the United States nor Europe has any right to oppose the Islamist movement if it expressed through the ballot box, as it did in Algeria, the will of the majority of the people. It is very likely that Islamism will win and it may be a necessary stage in some countries. Equally, I think it will become more moderate in other countries if their economic situation improves and political power is freed up. History will reveal one day if it can satisfy the material and moral aspirations of the societies that come to it for sustenance and guidance: whether it is merely a leap backward into the past or contains the seeds of access to economic, political, technological, and cultural modernity.

Eventual failure would strip it of its legitimacy and it would be up to those who hoisted it to power to draw their conclusions and repair the damage. We should always remember, as those intellectuals signatories to the Carthage Declaration reminded us (22 September, 1994) that "the grandeur of Muslim civilization is based on pluralism, hybridity, questioning, exploration and exchange. Only a return to these values can renew its greatness."

In the meantime, we should learn to respect the much that is worthy of respect in that great civilization contiguous to our own and to repudiate acts that violate international law and human rights whether they occur in the Muslim world or in the West, in Bosnia or in Algeria.